Angel Numbers

Also by Kyle Gray

Books

Angel Prayers
Connecting with the Angels Made Easy
Light Warrior
Raise Your Vibration
Wings of Forgiveness
Angels Whisper in My Ear

Audiobooks

Light Warrior
Raise Your Vibration
Angel Prayer Meditations

Card Decks

Angels and Ancestors Oracle Cards
Keepers of the Light Oracle Cards
Angel Prayers Oracle Cards

Online Courses

Certified Angel Guide
Connecting with the Angels Made Easy

Angel Numbers

The Message and Meaning Behind 11:11 and Other Number Sequences

KYLE GRAY

HAY HOUSE INDIA
New Delhi • London • Sydney
Carlsbad, California • New York City

Hay House Publishers (India) Pvt Ltd
Muskaan Complex, Plot No. 3, B-2, Vasant Kunj, New Delhi – 110 070, India

Hay House LLC, P.O. Box 5100, Carlsbad, CA 92018-5100, USA
Hay House UK Ltd, The Sixth Floor, Watson House, 54 Baker Street, London W1U 7BU, UK
Hay House Australia Publishing Pty Ltd, 18/36 Ralph St., Alexandria NSW 2015, Australia

Email: contact@hayhouse.co.in
Website: www.hayhouse.co.in

First published by Hay House India, 2020
Reprint, 2024
20 19 18 17 16 15 14 13 12 11

ISBN 978-93-88302-34-0

Printed at Repro India Ltd

FSC
www.fsc.org
MIX
Paper from responsible sources
FSC® C047271

Hay House is committed to a sustainable future for our business, our readers and our planet. This book is made from Forest Stewardship Council® certified paper.

Thank you, angels, for reminding the world of your presence.

Contents

Introduction

Angels are real. I had to start out by saying that, although you probably know it already. For thousands of years these divine beings have been making their presence known to those who walk the Earth.

In fact, since time began, people in all four corners of the world have believed in divine beings who connect this realm with the next, help people with everyday tasks and challenges, and support souls in crossing over when they're ready to return to the spirit realm. Aboriginal tribes painted them on the walls of caves, depicting them with big light-covered faces, large eyes, and halos of light surrounding their heads. In Japanese Shintoism today there are beings of grace and compassion known as *kami*, who are said to move through the air "as if they have wings" and to be forces of nature that are able to help those who call on them. There are similar beings in Tibetan Buddhism called *bodhisattvas*—beings of pure compassion who are dedicated to helping all those who call on them to overcome suffering and be free of their deepest fears. Robert Thurman, Professor of Indo-Tibetan Buddhist Studies at Columbia University in New York, describes *bodhisattvas* as "the Archangelic beings of Buddhism."

In almost every spiritual and religious tradition there is a similar force of love and light, though it takes many different forms. In India there are deities with the faces of animals, the wings of birds and the bodies of humans. The Hebrew Bible relates how the prophet Ezekiel had a vision of an angelic being with the faces of a child, a bull, a lion, and an eagle. Such beings were later described as "spheres of fire" (what we call "orbs" today) and "the Burning Ones," I think because at the time they didn't have electric light and the common way to light something up was through fire.

In my opinion, the way angels have appeared over the years has been perfectly in line with people's knowledge, experience, understanding, and beliefs at the time, wherever they have been in the world. And although there's no hard scientific evidence to prove these beings exist, basic sociology has shown that belief in divine messengers passing between the realms was common worldwide way before long-distance communication was even possible.

Today, belief in angels is getting even stronger. In 2016 a survey of 2,000 Britons revealed that one third believed in angels and 1 in 10 believed they had encountered an angel, and recent polls in the USA have shown that 8 in 10 Americans believe in angels. This is so exciting!

It's no wonder that so many of us are receiving what can only be described as signs and messages from heaven at this time, because these beings want us to know that they are here for us.

Some of these messages are coming through numbers. For thousands of years numbers have been considered auspicious and a way of understanding the universe. The ancient Greek philosopher Pythagoras believed that numbers had vibrational values that corresponded to those of musical notes. He created a system that was able to reveal information about a person's personality and outer expression based solely on the numerical values of their name, date, and place of birth. This system is referred to as Pythagorean Numerology.

In contrast, modern-day numerology focuses on the numerological values of your name (to reveal your destiny number) and date of birth (to reveal your life path number). Through the information revealed a person may understand their sense of calling toward a particular purpose, why certain personality traits are stronger than others, and what challenges they are here to face during this lifetime.

Although angel numbers and the Key Codex (*see page 12*) revealed in this book may contain similar ideas and information to Pythagorean Numerology, the information about each angel number in this book is divinely inspired and channelled rather than calculated.

Using the information revealed in this book you can combine angel numbers with numerology to help gain a more spiritual perspective around the calling of your soul and how the angels want to support you on your life journey.

As someone who has studied spirituality for the last 16 years, I have spent a lot of time looking into the true meaning of numbers. My conclusions have been influenced heavily by my years studying the Tarot and the Western mystery tradition. When I came to write this book, I also spent a great deal of time in meditation, inviting angels to reveal to me the messages and vibrational values of particular numbers. This has helped shape the interpretations I am presenting to you here.

In this day and age, our understanding of the cosmos and how the Earth is moving through it is all calculated using numbers, so it's no wonder that angels, the universe's greatest messengers, are using them to send us messages from the heavens.

For example, there's a good chance you have seen number sequences appearing time and time again in your life—on license plates, purchase receipts, flight numbers and of course your phone—and these numbers aren't just numbers, they're angel numbers. They are angel messages and calls to action.

Now that we are living in what can only be described as a digital age, angels are using the numbers we see on digital clocks, such as 11:11.

Seeing 11:11

I was a teenager when I first noticed 11:11 appearing everywhere I looked. I remember looking at my first cell phone and seeing it appearing time and time again. I wondered if I was going crazy, or imagining it, or even unconsciously looking at my phone at that particular time, but what happened next was undeniable: I told my mum and some of my friends about it, and it started happening when they were with me too. Other repeating number sequences kept appearing as well, and not just on cell phones. We'd go to the store for groceries and the bill would be £11.11, or we'd order coffee and cake, and it would come to £4.44. It was the same wherever I went.

I was fairly new to spirituality then, but I took some time to pray and ask about what was happening. I remember saying something like, "Angels, if it's you sending me these numbers, I want to see them three times today, so that I know you're trying to tell me something." And the numbers kept coming—I knew that angels *were* sending messages.

But what were they saying? I had no idea. I remember Googling "What does 11:11 mean?" and reading several interpretations. Many people said the numbers indicated that this was a time to "make a wish" or "set an intention," while others said they meant that angels were encouraging us to align our thoughts with the highest. So I did what I always do when Google doesn't have a definite answer: I meditated.

During my meditation I remember saying a simple prayer like: "Angels, thank you for revealing to me what I need to know about seeing 11:11," and in a flash I saw lots of images and scenes like movie clips in my mind, including images of Jesus and the Buddha, and heard the words "We are all one." As my vision continued, I saw Muslim friends praying to Mecca and again heard "We are all one." Then I saw a video of Bob Marley singing "One Love" and just felt encompassed by unity. I was one with angels, one with ascended masters and one with God!

So, 11:11 is a message we've received time and time again through the ages: it's a reminder that we are all one. We are interlaced and interconnected with the field of energy that creates and cultivates the universe.

But it doesn't end there. For me, this recurring message isn't just "You are one with all that is," and that's it. It's a *call to action*. It's almost as though the universe/God (same thing to me) is inviting us to be fully aware that the power and light of the universe are within us. Jesus said, "The Kingdom of Heaven is within you." So, if the power and light of the universe are within us, what we choose to do in our life affects that energy. And so 11:11 is a call to align ourselves, our intentions, and our actions with the highest. That's what it means to be a lightworker or an Earth angel.

Angels Always Have an Answer

Yet again angels had provided the answer. They always do. And just as we all have the power of the universe within us, we all have angels with us. I believe we all have at least two angels working with us at all times. There's the guardian angel that's been with us for lifetimes and there's at least one other angel as well, for different angels work with us at different times, depending on where we are on our journey and what we are working on or working through. Wherever we are, angels are there for us and love to guide us and support us. They always act in accordance with divine law, however, and so they generally cannot move into our life and help us unless they have our permission.

The only times angels can intervene on our behalf without permission are what I call "moments of Grace." Basically, these are when we are in a situation which could divert us from our highest goodness and truth, or when we have begun a life mission but not yet completed it and are in a life or death situation. It's at these moments that our angels can become our saving grace.

We don't have to be in such extreme circumstances to receive help from our angels, of course. Whenever we pray to them for guidance, they will have an answer. It's just that we might not hear it. I believe that this is because many of us haven't listened to ourselves for years, let alone anyone else, and have ignored the guidance that's been coming from within. Quite simply, angels are as loud as our willingness to listen. Or to look. Because now, as I mentioned earlier, they're using digital media to send us messages and reminders of their presence.

I have written about these number sequences in some of my other books, in particular *Raise Your Vibration*, which was actually inspired by my constant witnessing of the numbers 11:11 and 22:22. Now I have asked the angels to allow me to understand the messages and themes behind repetitive number sequences more deeply, so I can write about them here and you can gain insight into what angels are saying to you through numbers and receive the answers to your questions and prayers.

How to Use This Book

As a Guide

In this book, first of all I look at four-number sequences from digital clocks, such as those on your laptop or cell phone, and then I provide an interpretation of every number from 0 to 999.

If you can't find the exact number sequence you keep seeing, I recommend you break the number down into two or three groups and then look at the angel messages for each group and put them together. For example, if you are seeing 67891 everywhere, look at the messages for 67, 89, and 1 and put them together to get the full message.

Just in case you were wondering:

◊ 67: Your thoughts are directing the flow of energy and support in your life. Take time to align with the thoughts that are serving your expansion.

◊ 89: You are in touch with your true self. Cherish this connection as it unfolds.

◊ 1: The universal life-force within you is calling for your awareness and attention.

What an inspiring message. I hope all the messages here will inspire you. As you go through the book, you'll find that many are different from one another, but many are similar. That's because those number sequences represent different aspects of journeys that have a similar theme.

As you move forward on your own particular journey, different numbers may come to your attention. You may initially see 332, for example, and then 334. You'll see that 332's message is: "Your relationships are moving into a space of growth in order for you to feel content," and 334's message is: "Your guides and angels are circling around you, offering divine love and protection." So these two numbers could show you making progress on a journey to happiness.

You can also create your own interpretations of the numbers in your life using the key that the angels gave me (*see page 12*).

Say, for example, you are seeing 123 repetitively. This is a message that you are aligning with love and expanding on your journey. Try your own number sequences for yourself.

Angel Numbers Key Codex

0. New Beginnings. Doors opening. God.
1. The Self. Oneness. Higher Self. Universal connection.
2. Union. Connection to others. Aligning with love.
3. Expansion. Higher power. The Masters.
4. Angels. Communication. Gifts expanding.
5. Changes. Effort. Action and input required.
6. Balance. Intention required. Carefulness.
7. Magic. Manifestation. Divine Inspiration.
8. Journey. Growth. Spiritual lessons.
9. Self-mastery. Union with higher self. Divine feminine.

As an Oracle

The book you are holding in your hands is also an oracle. Any time you are in need of guidance or support, you can ask the angels listening in to send a message to you through it. All you have to do is spend some time in meditation and contemplation, center yourself with some deep breaths and say a simple prayer along the lines of:

Thank you, God, Holy Spirit, and angels,
for revealing a message of significance to me
through these numbers and this book today.

Open the book up at random and trust that the first number sequence you see is the message that you need to receive.

Why not try it now? Or look at a digital clock and then read on...

Digital Clock Number Messages

Here you'll find angel messages in the number sequences you'll most commonly see on a digital clock, though you may also see them elsewhere. (*If you're looking for a number sequence that isn't a digital clock time, please refer to the Key Codex on page 12 to decipher the angels' message to you.*)

Double and Triple Numbers

When you see double and triple numbers appearing on the clock, angels are in some way "shouting" to get your attention. These number sequences reveal your current energetic vibration and how your journey is unfolding.

Double Numbers

00:00

God is with you, supporting you as you take the steps necessary to grow.

01:01

God is close by and is helping you feel safe, supported, and connected to your intentions and endeavors.

02:02

You are being guided by God and angels to open your heart, mind, and energy to the support of those surrounding you.

03:03

God and ascended masters are drawing close to support your deeper understanding of your soul and the expansion of your journey.

04:04

God and angels are supporting you in sharing your truth, gifts, and self with the world.

05:05

Know that God is helping you with all of your material and financial needs. Ask and you shall receive.

06:06

You are being guided by God and angels to make space in your life for balance and the restoration of your energy.

07:07

God is surrounding you with the angels and guardians of magic so that you can step into your power to create and experience the life that you deserve.

08:08

Trust that God is helping you align with the divine plan, which will take your intentions into consideration as well as what is best for your soul's expansion.

09:09

God is guiding you to reveal the deeper, more vulnerable aspects of yourself. This will open you up to miracles and light!

10:10

You are on the cusp of something miraculous. Trust that God and angels are one and are with you now.

11:11

You are one with God, angels, and ascended masters. Align your thoughts with the highest goodness and truth in order to bring love into the world.

12:12

You have the power to bring healing and light to the world. Notice how your intentions and actions are already doing just that.

13:13

To teach is to learn. There are many important lessons in your current situation. Make a note of whatever you heal, for you will teach others to do it too.

14:14

Your angels are offering strong support at this time, helping you reconnect with any talents you have forgotten or aspects of your being that have been discouraged in the past.

15:15

Know that the changes you are making at this time are necessary in order for you to grow. Trust that the space you are making is creating room for abundance.

16:16

Take time to find balance in your life. You are being encouraged to slow down and consider your intentions carefully before proceeding further.

17:17

You are magical! Whatever concerns or blocks you have been experiencing are now being released so you can turn your dreams into reality.

18:18

You are embarking on a life-changing journey. The outcome will be positive and enriching experiences. Trust the process.

19:19

You are being invited to connect with the energy of the divine feminine both within you and around you. Mother/feminine healing is possible at this time.

20:20

There's an opportunity for you to strengthen your connection with others. The energies of forgiveness and compassion are surrounding both personal and professional relationships.

21:21

Realize that the other person is also you. You are one with the world and the intentions you have for others are also the intentions you have for yourself. Upgrade your thoughts.

22:22

You have power and gifts that will light up the world. Focus on the highest good. You were born to shine.

23:23

Your focus on expanding and becoming a positive force in the world are paying off. Angels want you to know that you are one of them upon the Earth.

Triple Numbers

1:11

Your thoughts and intentions are magnified at this time. Focus on what you love, not what you fear.

2:22

Your gifts are creating opportunities for you to expand. Be open to opportunities that will enable you to fulfill your purpose.

3:33

All of the great spiritual teachers of the past are guiding you at this time. These ascended masters are helping you develop your gifts.

4:44

Your guardian angels want you to know that they are with you. Your prayers are being heard loud and clear. Have faith.

5:55

All of your efforts are now paying off. Know that the universe and your angels are supporting you in creating and living an abundant life.

Mirror Numbers

These are numbers that appear reflected back as if there's a mirror between them. Their messages usually call for you to reflect on your current circumstances in order to become more aligned with what will support your growth.

12:21

You can support and guide others, so angels are reminding you not to burn out or to skip self-care on your journey as a lightworker.

13:31

You are being invited to revisit your current circumstances in order to re-evaluate your opportunities to learn and grow.

14:41

Your angels are communicating, but you aren't listening. It's important to know that their messages are always given for the highest good. Even if they don't seem to be in line with your plans, know that they are following God's plan.

15:51

Your angels are encouraging you to be brave and strong. It's important for you to see where changes are required in order to feel aligned with purpose and abundance.

Progressing Numbers

Progressing numbers are numbers that move upward in correct sequence. When you see numbers like this, angels are acknowledging that you are rising up and moving forward on your path. Ultimately, they see you embarking on the journey to ascension by successfully raising your vibration.

12:34

You are moving up the spiritual ladder. Your angels are acknowledging your intentions and your steps toward growth. Know that you are being encouraged and supported.

1:23

You are moving up a step. All the challenges you have previously experienced are now being released. The angels of ascension are with you.

2:34

Your personal relationships are growing at this time. Know that you are receiving opportunities to love and be loved like never before. Your angels are dancing around you.

3:45

Ascended masters are with you and your guides to help elevate your spiritual connection. Trust in the feelings you are having—they are the answers to your prayers.

4:56

Angels want you to know that they are so glad about your current commitment to your spiritual growth. You will feel a sense of acceleration at this time.

Angel Numbers 0–999

0

God is close by. You are never alone.

1

The universal life-force within you is calling for your attention.

2

There are opportunities for connection and union at this time. Relationship growth is imminent.

3

You are on the road to growth and expansion. The path is unfolding with perfect timing.

4

Let your truth be your teacher. Trust in all that you feel and let your joy lead.

5

Abundance is a state of mind. When you feel rich spiritually, your physical life will reflect it.

6

Take time to eliminate all that's blocking your joy. Follow what makes your heart dance.

7

The energy of magic is surrounding you. Align your thoughts with the highest.

8

A cycle or pattern is being repeated now so that you understand the lesson. Take time to reflect.

9

The energy of the divine is awakening within you. Let your soul do the leading.

10

You are uniting your energy with that of God. Trust that the signs you are seeing are direct communication with the divine.

11

You are in a state of expansion and getting to know your true self better than ever. Know you were born to shine.

12

All relationships are assignments. You are finding your friends and your tribe, and even understanding soul-mate relationships at this time.

13

Trust that the steps on your path are unfolding as they should and are serving your expansion.

14

Your angels are encouraging you to spend time listening to them. Remember, angels are as loud as your willingness to listen.

15

Your changing thoughts are changing your life. Align your awareness and energy with thoughts that lift you.

16

You are being invited to upgrade your choices and move toward experiences that support your joy and purpose. Let go and move forward.

17

As one door closes, another door opens. Angels are with you to help direct your thoughts in a positive way.

18

Your angels are encouraging you to take an inventory of your past experiences in order to understand your current position and lessons.

19

It's okay for you to be powerful. You are being guided by heaven to take ownership of your current situation.

20

Your angels are congratulating you on taking steps toward growth and expansion. You have a deeper connection to your soul now.

21

Your connection to the universe is really strong and you are being filled with inspiration and guidance. Be open and aware.

22

You are at a crucial point on your journey which will help you understand the relationships and spiritual assignments that will support your growth.

23

You are being guided by ascended masters at this time. Trust that the path you are on is perfect for your current situation.

24

Angels are shining a light of harmony on you and your personal relationships. Any conflicts are now being resolved.

25

Your angels want you to trust that all your hard work and commitment will pay off. Soon you will enjoy the fruits of your labor.

26

It's important for you to be in the company of people who lift your spirit. Step back from anyone who is making you feel small.

27

You are being given signs that your prayers are being heard. Trust that God's plan is unfolding as it needs to.

28

Your angels want to give you a high five, as they recognize your commitment to being a light in the world. Well done for facing your fears.

29

Powerful Goddess and Divine Mother energy is surrounding you. You are being enveloped in love and compassion.

30

You are here for a reason. Know that your happiness has a purpose and is of service to the world.

31

Saints and masters are working closely with your prayers and intentions at this time. Know they are doing their best to help you.

32

Your relationships—with yourself and others—are being supported by your angels and guides. Call on them for as much help as you need, and know it's never too much.

33

Master Jesus and his angels are with you. This is a sacred time for growth and healing.

34

You are being connected to universal masters for inspiration and insights that will guide you on your journey. Trust in your feelings.

35

Your angels and guides are ready to support you through any changes you need to make to be more at ease.

36

There are opportunities for you to increase your enjoyment of your career at this time and raise your level of abundance. Your guides are ready to help.

37

The masters of manifestation are surrounding you and helping you create the life you have always dreamed of.

38

You are uncovering memories from lifetimes beyond your current lifetime—your current spiritual interests are inspired by experiences from previous lives.

39

The divine feminine within you is so grateful that you are listening to your soul's voice.

40

God and angels are with you now. Have no fear.

41

Your angels are encouraging you to embrace your gifts and know that you are worthy of having them.

42

Angels are lovingly guiding you to express your emotions. Align yourself with truth and integrity.

43

Angels, your loved ones, and guides and masters who can support you, are all with you now. Know that help is only a thought away.

44

Your guardian angel is wrapping you in a cloak of loving protection. You are safe.

45

Archangel Michael and the other archangels are standing with you in solidarity and strength.

46

Trust that archangels are supporting you through the energy of change that is around you at this time.

47

The angels of manifestation are helping you align your energy and thoughts with what is going to be of most service to you.

48

The angels of purpose are with you now, helping you understand and follow the truth and purpose that will light you up.

49

Angels are helping you embrace the emotions that are rising up within you at this time. Look on your emotions as messengers.

50

A strong energy of abundance is with you at this time. Think big and focus on the energy of plenty.

51

Within you, you have everything you need to overcome roadblocks. Now is the time to face your fears and grow.

52

Challenging conversations will take you to a place of certainty and understanding. Be open to hearing the truth.

53

The universe is never working against you, it's always working for you. Trust in God's plan as it unfolds.

54

Your angels are encouraging you to move into a state of surrender so that they are able to help you move forward.

55

Major shifts are taking place in your finances and state of abundance. Know that opportunities to soar are coming your way.

56

Take time to assess what you can give in order to receive. Energy always works in the form of exchange.

57

Belief makes manifest. Imagine what you are asking for is already in your hands ... and life.

58

The bumps on your journey are now being ironed out. Know that the worst of this situation is over.

59

There's a chance for you to undertake major spiritual growth at this time. Open up to healing information.

60

Your angels are guiding you to slow down and take time to reflect before making any sudden changes.

61

Your angels are inviting you to preserve your energy for projects and events that light you up. Move away from drama.

62

Take time to see the points of view of those you may be challenged by at this time. Call on the angels of harmony to ease any challenging relationships.

63

Releasing situations that are draining will make room for miracles and expansion. Take time to release the old.

64

Your angels are inviting you to spend more time in contemplation and meditation so that they can strengthen the communication channels between you.

65

Your finances are a reflection of your self-worth. Know that God sees you as deserving of blessings and harmony.

66

Halt. Do not make any sudden moves or changes. Your angels are inviting you to consider your next steps carefully.

67

Your thoughts are directing the flow of energy and support in your life. Take time to align with the thoughts that are serving your expansion.

68

You may feel as though you are being blocked, but know that your angels are redirecting you toward your long-term goals.

69

Sensitivity is a gift. Know that your emotions are helping you tap into the real and important aspects of your being.

70

Cosmic energy is surrounding you at this time. Know that God is waiting for your intentions to be clear in order to support their manifestation.

71

You are being invited to get clear about what you want instead of focusing on what you don't want. Write down your intentions and allow God in to help.

72

It's important to reconnect with yourself and your internal world in order to experience more clarity in your external world.

73

Blocks are now being cleared. You are being aligned with magic.

74

Angels want you to spend more time sharing your plans with them so they are better able to support you.

75

In order for your intentions to manifest you must be prepared to embrace the energy of change. New beginnings are imminent.

76

Take time to embrace your fears and realize that when you are plagued by fear, you are on the verge of a miracle.

77

Prepare for the best. Good news is coming and positive changes are unfolding.

78

Your personal journey is unfolding perfectly. Trust in the process.

79

Your higher self has information that can support you. Call up the teacher you have within.

80

You are here to make a difference. Your experiences haven't happened by accident. Trust and believe in your story.

81

Angels are helping you understand repeating stories and patterns in your life so you can assess and overcome challenges.

82

There is an opportunity for you to go on your own journey. Don't let the opinions of others stand in the way of your dreams.

83

Look on every mistake you have made as an opportunity to learn and grow. Let go of regret.

84

The angels of forgiveness are drawing close to help you release past situations and embrace the lessons within them.

85

You were not born to suffer. Move beyond expecting a negative outcome.

86

Your current lesson is to step back from anything that is making you feel low or drained.

87

You are a teacher and you can share the knowledge you have gained from your experiences.

88

There's a portal opening up for you to step into a more spiritually centered life.

89

You are in touch with your true self. Cherish this connection as it unfolds.

90

The best relationship you'll ever have is your relationship with yourself. Say "No" to others and "Yes" to yourself.

91

Your angels are proud of your commitment to your growth.

92

Your energy is paving the way for joyful and fun experiences to come to you.

93

Your higher self requires you to extend your meditation time in order to upgrade your energy system.

94

Your angels' messages are coming through your intuition at this time. Trust what you feel.

95

The universe knows exactly what steps to present to you. Surrender to the experience.

96

Your angels are encouraging you to slow down, as this will open up windows and doors to opportunity.

97

You are a magnet for all things at this time. Align your energy with golden thoughts and golden energy to attract golden opportunities.

98

Your intentions and efforts are creating a new way forward for you.

99

You are having an enlightened moment. Take note of all that is coming through to you at this time.

100

Your angels are congratulating you on all of the hard work you are doing. You are a special light on the Earth.

101

God is within and is listening closely to all of your prayers and intentions.

102

Take time to know that the stronger your relationship with yourself, the stronger your connections will be with God, angels, and others.

103

Know that God sees you as a divine and worthy child of light.

104

God and angels are with you every step of the way. Call on them for help when you need it. Never feel alone.

105

God and angels are with you now to help with your situation regarding finances and security. Make way for miracles.

106

In order to move forward, you are being guided to cut all the cords that are binding you to the situations of the past.

107

Your thoughts and intentions are manifesting before you. Believe and you will receive.

108

You are on a journey that is leading inward. You have all the answers you are seeking.

109

Know that the divine is within you. Your angels are focusing on your holiness.

110

You are being inspired and led by God and angels.

111

You are one with all that is. Know that all you are doing and giving is for the world and all the beings in it.

112

You are being encouraged to look at the higher purpose behind all the current relationships in your life.

113

Masters, saints, and higher-being teachers are with you now, helping you move forward in faith on your journey.

114

Your angels want to thank you for being one of them upon the Earth. You have a real gift for healing.

115

Your thoughts are manifesting radically now, so it's important to stay aligned with the thoughts you know will serve your expansion.

116

It's important for you to think outside the box and beyond your current situation before making choices and moving forward.

117

Your angels are waiting for you to make your intentions clear. Get clear about what you want.

118

In order to grow you have to let go of attachments to the outcome of a situation, especially if it involves others. Take time to refocus your energy on your own path.

119

You are being invited to step into your power and take charge of your situation. Stop waiting for other people to influence your next move.

120

Your angels can see you intend to do and be your best. Know that they are giving you a boost of loving encouragement.

121

The universe is here, right here with you. Know that you are more connected to it than ever.

122

You are at a very important stage of your journey, so it's important to stay mindful and present.

123

You are moving up a step. All the challenges you have previously experienced are now being released. The angels of ascension are with you now.

124

Your angels are reminding you never to think of anyone or anything as more spiritual or more connected than you are. Reclaim your holiness.

125

Your angels are encouraging you to know that you have always done everything to the best of your knowledge and experience.

126

When you are facing a roadblock or something is going "wrong," trust that God has a better plan for you.

127

The signs that you are seeing are to let you know that you are on the right path and that it's the path of light.

128

You are rising up and flying at this time. Know that your angels are there to embrace you as you soar into an experience of love and abundance.

129

The Divine Mother is with you with her loving and nurturing light. Know that you are loved beyond your comprehension.

130

Choose to live with purpose and to take steps that you know will serve you and your expansion.

131

Saints and holy masters are with you at this time. They can see that you have a real capacity to help the world heal and be embraced by light.

132

Your angels are inviting you to spend time connecting to your own energy and listening to your body at this time. There are messages to uncover.

133

Jesus and holy masters are guiding you now. Darkness is being brought into the light—it's time to expect miracles.

134

Healing angels are gathering around you and will guide you to the information that will take you forward.

135

Trust that the changes unfolding now are taking you closer to your initial intentions and goals.

136

Your career or purpose is presenting you with new opportunities. Know that God and angels are behind every choice that is best for your wellbeing.

137

You have manifesting energy with you at this time. Believe that what you need is already with and within you.

138

Your angels and guides are encouraging you to forgive and release the past so that you can manifest a more fulfilling future.

139

It's important to surround yourself with a powerful bevy of women at this time. The divine feminine is the answer you need in your current situation.

140

You are one with God and angels. Stand strong.

141

Archangels are shielding and protecting you now.

142

Your guardian angel is swirling around you with love and acceptance. You are loved. You are accepted.

143

You have known your guardian angel for lifetimes. Meditate and ask your soul to reveal helpful memories.

144

A hundred thousand angels are enveloping you in their light and love.

145

Archangels are inviting you to open up and reclaim your gifts in order to receive their messages.

146

You are in a state of transition. Know that angels are guiding you through the process.

147

Your angels are helping you turn your dreams into reality. Be clear about your intentions and open up your heart to receive.

148

Your angels can only help you experience miracles if you believe they are possible. Know that they *are* possible, and for you.

149

Your emotions are a real part of your being. Connecting with them will help you grow.

150

Powerful opportunities are coming. They will present you with excitement and stability.

151

Your confidence is growing and will encourage your gifts and talents to surface. Continue to trust in yourself.

152

Taking time to review the higher purpose behind challenges will allow you to move forward fearlessly.

153

Your increasing trust in the universe is allowing it to present you with miraculous solutions to your challenges. Continue to trust.

154

Trust in your inner voice, as it's providing you with angelically inspired wisdom at this time.

155

You are a master of manifestation and your visions are becoming reality.

156

Move beyond the limitations and negative patterns of others and never doubt your kindness and your capacity to give. You are kind because it's who you are.

157

When the past comes back to visit, it's so you can let it go and make room to grow. Surrender and release.

158

The universe is redirecting you to a pathway that is more in line with your intentions and goals. Accept the changes that are coming your way.

159

Your angels are guiding you toward information and people that will help you uncover deeper aspects of your journey. Open your mind to new pathways.

160

God is as loud as your willingness to listen. Do everything you can to listen … deeply.

161

The light to put an end to all darkness is shining strongly within you at this time. You are the light.

162

Your angels are guiding you to be the peaceful one in your current situation. Hold the light.

163

Open your heart to love and let it in.

164

Your angels are helping you to see from a higher perspective.

165

You are being guided to be open to new possibilities.

166

It's important to reconsider your current options. Your angels are inviting you to realign your intentions with the highest good.

167

Your acts of love and self-care are opening your world to more love and blessings.

168

Your angel team is inviting you to stop spreading yourself so thin. Streamline your focus and intentions for a desirable outcome.

169

Taking time to connect with and honor your emotions is important at this time. Your angels adore you.

170

You are in a powerful magnetic place right now. To create opportunities, focus lovingly on your plans.

171

Your angels are reminding you about the power of your prayers. Know that they can create miracles.

172

Your angels and your own energy are helping you to know who is trustworthy in your world and to connect with them.

173

Your angels are with you to help you remember you are worthy of miracles.

174

Angels are encouraging you to call back your power and take charge of your current situation.

175

The changes you are experiencing are occurring according to your will. Trust that the universe is adjusting your steps accordingly.

176

The universe is inviting you to be clear about your intentions, as they are not clear at this time. Open up a dialogue with God.

177

Your intentions are being heard loud and clear. God is guiding you.

178

Trust that you are being led to the perfect opportunities to display your gifts.

179

Your psychic abilities and awareness are developing rapidly. Meditate regularly to connect with your gifts.

180

Nothing is happening by chance. Know that your life here is for a purpose—a higher purpose.

181

You are being invited to leave behind challenging situations of the past in order to prepare yourself for miracles.

182

Your angels are encouraging you to let go of other people's challenges, mistakes, and bad behavior. You deserve to be free of them.

183

Your angels and guides are with you to help you review your life and to encourage you to see how far you have come on the journey of growth.

184

Forgiveness is a gift you give to yourself. Know that you are worthy of freedom from the past.

185

Angels want you to know that they adore you.

186

Take time to review your current situation before making any life-changing decisions. Patience and focus are required.

187

What you have experienced and what you have learned are gifts that allow you to understand who you are and what talents you have. Take time to see that you are a special soul.

188

You are one with your consciousness and the universe at this time. You are one with your gifts, dreams, and goals. Believe.

189

Your third eye is opening and your spiritual sight is sharpening. See through the eyes of your soul.

190

Return home to yourself and go into the cave of your heart, where your guardian angel is waiting to receive your unconditional love.

191

You are not imagining the messages you are receiving—angels are speaking to you loud and clear.

192

You are being encouraged to be more present in your relationships at this time. Your loved ones need your attention.

193

Your soul is growing as a result of your current situation. Soak up every experience and know that angels are there to hold you.

194

Angels want you to know that you have an opportunity to increase your sense of purpose. Be open to new ideas.

195

Your gifts require your attention if they are to develop. Take time to dive deep within and study yourself and the gifts you have.

196

Reconnecting with your initial intentions will allow you to understand your current placement within the universe.

197

Grace is a quality of spirit. Your angels are encouraging you to be graceful in your words, actions, and intentions.

198

You are experiencing important soul lessons at this time. It's important to pray for guidance to overcome repeating patterns.

199

Welcome to the cave of your heart. You have arrived at the center of your being.

200

You are here to make a difference in the hearts of many. You are a gift to the world. God has your back.

201

Thank you for trusting the light within you. Your angels are pleased that you are recognizing your holiness.

202

God is guiding you to know yourself more deeply.

203

Your commitment to growth is inspiring and lifting the vibration of all those around you.

204

You are here to speak truth and share love. Know that God is with you wherever you are.

205

Seeing yourself at one with your wildest dreams allows them to unfold gracefully in your life.

206

Ensure that your intentions are not influencing or interfering with the free will of others.

207

The magic you need is within you.

208

In order to move forward and grow, you have to come face to face with the truth. Get real with yourself.

209

You are here to grace the world with your presence. You are lighting up your corner of the world.

210

God and angels are welcoming you back to your truth. You are reconnecting with the pathway that is right for you.

211

You are in a powerful place at this time, aligning with great minds of the past and present. Focus on your dreams and the highest good.

212

This is an important time for you to reflect on who you are and who you want to bring to your relationships, and ultimately the world.

213

Don't be afraid—that feeling of being held back is just the universe recalibrating itself on your behalf. Trust the process.

214

Your relationship with angels is stronger than ever.

215

You are in a space to overcome your fears. Have faith—you are moving through this in order to move up!

216

Your angels are inviting you to see yourself through their holiest and most loving eyes. See your beauty inside and out.

217

You are being reminded that the energy of those around you affects your vibrational state. Choose who you connect with accordingly.

218

You are being encouraged to take a leap of faith and trust what lights you up!

219

Know that your relationships with others require your peaceful and loving leadership. Take time to share your intentions for growth.

220

Show up for yourself and you show up for the world.

221

You are being guided by your angels to face the darkest aspects of your life in order to bring more light to your current situation and to the world.

222

You have the ability to lift up the hearts of all those around you like an angel on the Earth. You were born to shine.

223

Ascended masters and your guides and angels are all encouraging you to be honest with yourself before proceeding further.

224

Your angels are guiding you. Trust that harmony is being delivered now.

225

You are an agent of change and the actions you have taken recently are in accordance with the divine plan. Everything is unfolding in the perfect time–space sequence.

226

Remember that whatever is missing in a relationship is yours to bring to it. Don't focus on the problem, be the solution.

227

God and angels have heard your prayers and are working to deliver the solution that is best for everyone involved in the current situation.

228

The universe is reminding you that your journey and experiences are led by your intentions and prayers. Get focused on your desired outcome to experience it.

229

The divine is encouraging you to align your choices, thoughts, and intentions with the highest good so that your experiences can be aligned with purpose and abundance.

230

Your purpose is to be happy. Your angels are encouraging you to do what makes your heart sing.

231

It may feel as though you have taken a step backward, but this diversion is being orchestrated by a team of angels who are working together for your highest good. Trust in the process.

232

You are seeing the truth, and your angels are encouraging you to trust in and act on that truth.

233

Ascended masters, in particular Jesus, are with you now to help you take the steps that will lead to your highest good. Call in all the help you need.

234

You are moving upward. The universe is proud of your commitment to growth.

235

Shifts are occurring that will bring you a greater sense of contentment and peace.

236

You are here to enjoy yourself and live with joy. Your angels are encouraging you to relax and let go, as this will increase the positive energy in your life.

237

Your dreams are blooming rapidly before your eyes. Continue with your loving focus and intentions.

238

You have been here before and your connection to spirit has been a part of many lifetimes. You are here now to be a beacon of light and strength.

239

The divine feminine, in the form of all the female deities, saints, and masters, is here to help you reconnect with the deepest aspects of your being. The truth is not out there, but within.

240

Know that God and angels are standing with you at this time. Be open to change.

241

Your angels are guiding you to reclaim your gifts. Stop putting yourself down and see your talents.

242

Angels see you through the eyes of unconditional love. Know that you are loved beyond measure.

243

Don't be alarmed if you are feeling low. You are processing energy in order to raise your vibration.

244

Angels are taking you to the next level. It's time to feel worthy!

245

Archangels are with you to help you cut the cords that are holding you back. Clear, cancel, and delete the past.

246

There's an opportunity to bring loving balance to your life and energy at this time. It requires work and effort, but hang on in there.

247

Cosmic gateway. Your thoughts are magnetic and powerful. Trust the changes that are occurring—they are miracles.

248

You are at a pivotal point on your life path. Opportunities to step into your purpose are being presented to you now.

249

Your angels are guiding you to unleash your spirit. Express your true and most sacred self.

250

Your commitment to your path and your devotion to change will be rewarded.

251

Your angels are encouraging you to trust in the guidance that is rising up within you—it's divinely led.

252

You are in a place where the relationship you have with yourself will be lovingly reflected in the relationships you have with others.

253

Sometimes the greatest abundance is found in recovering the lost parts of yourself. Welcome yourself home.

254

Your angels are encouraging you to love yourself enough to communicate your feelings about your current situation.

255

Doors to abundance and opportunity are swinging open. It's time to stand in the spotlight and shine.

256

In order to receive, you must be prepared to give and share. Move beyond a limiting and lacking mindset.

257

Remember that you are one with the divine and all that is, so all that you are seeking is already one with you.

258

Make the choice that brings you closest to *your* joy and your path will unfold effortlessly.

259

You are connected to divine guidance and the inspiration you are receiving is real.

260

Take time to offer your presence to your family and loved ones. They need you.

261

It's important to show up for a partner, as they need you at this time.

262

You are being invited to be honest with yourself and in your relationships.

263

God and angels are welcoming you back. You may have wandered from your path for a while, but you are certainly reconnected.

264

Your angels are reminding you that it's okay to be human. They love who you are and who you have become.

265

You are being invited to show up for yourself the way you show up for others.

266

Speak to yourself lovingly. God is always listening.

267

Open your heart and energy to experience abundance.

268

Find a sense of contentment with where you are on your journey. Enjoy the blessings of the here and now.

269

Connecting with the heart of a situation will guide you lovingly to the solution you are seeking. Choose to act and react from the highest aspect of your being.

270

God is here and wants to give to you. Let yourself believe that you are worthy of this divine love.

271

The next step on your path is down to you. Get clear in your heart about where you want this road to go.

272

The key to abundance and manifesting at this time is reconnecting with your heart and all that you love. This will lift you to the highest vibration.

273

You are being guided to connect with your inner fire and inner strength in order to move back into a state of wholeness.

274

Your angels are your biggest cheerleaders and they are with you every step of the way. Rise up and move beyond all drama.

275

The changes you are experiencing are the steps necessary for your intentions to manifest. Trust.

276

You will be strengthened when you remember you are never alone. God is with and within you always.

277

The universe is with you. Rise up and honor your inner force.

278

Your life is destined for greatness. Remain focused on your purpose.

279

You are being asked to move beyond current challenges in order to rise up. This is a time when you will turn what feels like lead into gold.

280

Trust in the path that is unfolding before you. All is happening as it needs to.

281

Your angels are reminding you that your life is in your hands. Take back your power.

282

A powerful lesson in assertiveness and authenticity is unfolding for you. Speak up and be heard.

283

You are being guided to move into a state of care and compassion. Choose to be love.

284

Your angels are encouraging you to do what is right. Step into service and know that your own pathway will be served by it.

285

Your angels are encouraging you to trust in the wisdom that is within you. Trust in what you know. You do have the answers.

286

Your angels are encouraging you to retreat in order to recharge. Divine healing is surrounding you.

287

You are on the path of light, love, and forgiveness. Stand in the light and manifest your future from a loving space.

288

Magic is manifesting all around you. Trust that your dreams and visions are becoming reality.

289

Reclaim your truth. Reclaim who you are. Know you are here to rise high.

290

Take charge and lead by example. God is walking with you.

291

Angels and the Holy Spirit are with you. Remember that only love is real.

292

Miracles are unfolding before your eyes. Prepare for a shift of perception and reality.

293

You are now moving beyond your limitations into a space of support. You are protected by divine power.

294

Your angels are lovingly whispering guidance through your heart space. Go within, listen, and connect to their love.

295

There are divine downloads within you that you need to open in order to move forward on your path.

296

Love is yours. Recognize your divine worth. Start by seeing yourself with loving eyes.

297

Focus on your intentions and trust in the power of heaven. You are being supported by a troop of angels.

298

Stand strong. Focus on your purpose and your path will unfold before you. You are here to overcome the fear of persecution.

299

The divine truth within you is powerful and here to light up the world.

300

God, ascended masters, and angels are here to bless your path with sheer light.

301

You are in a powerful space of alignment at this time. Don't let anything interrupt your flow and spiritual connection.

302

You are growing personally and professionally. Keep your energy high and focus on making a difference.

303

God is sending guides and holy masters to support you. Let the light in.

304

Angels are swirling around you, inviting you to raise your thoughts, intentions, and energy to the highest vibration possible.

305

Face your challenges so that you can make changes rather than have changes presented to you. Unite with honesty and integrity.

306

Call in your angels and ask them to help you stay balanced and focused on priorities.

307

You are the miracle. You are the magic. Everything that you touch at this time will turn to gold.

308

Your spiritual growth is accelerating. You may notice your guides changing as you rise up.

309

Your higher self is guiding you at this time. Dive deep within and be open to new directions.

310

You are one with your higher power. Know that you are loved and supported.

311

Your energy and presence are gifts to the world. Your awareness is open and aligned with the oneness of life.

312

You are being invited to recognize the growth that is taking place in your relationships at this time. Know that no connection happens by accident.

313

Emerge from the cave. Let your light be seen. You are here to learn and to teach.

314

Angels are encouraging you to shine your light and trust in it.

315

The changes you are seeing are the answers to your prayers. Trust that the next steps on your path will be delivered to you.

316

Make more room for miracles in your life. Find time to just be.

317

Your dedication to growth is opening the doors to magic. Remember that with power comes responsibility.

318

Your commitment to the journey of expansion is being recognized. The angels of direction and support are traveling with you.

319

Your presence is your power. Show up and let all of your shields down, knowing that the divine is the only shield you need.

320

You have a direct connection with God. Let yourself be loved—you are entitled to a personal relationship with your divine parent.

321

You are not on the wrong path, but you are being guided to let the divine take over from here. Surrender to its power.

322

You are being invited to remember that as it's you who's on this spiritual journey, you have to take the lead when light and resolution are required. Forgive.

323

Ascended masters are with you to remove all blockages and challenges on your pathway so that you can live fearlessly.

324

Your angel squad has your back and you are only a prayer away from help.

325

Make space in your life for support. You need to be supported by God and your angels in order to support others.

326

Don't let the low vibrations or dramas of others block your light. Instead, surround yourself with those who lift you up.

327

Your plan for your life must be aligned with the highest good. If it is, then God's plan will align with yours and will deliver your wishes.

328

Your devotion to growth has been recognized. Ask and you shall receive.

329

You are aligned with the power and presence of the Divine Mother. Know that you are loved.

330

Angels and ascended masters want you to know that God believes in you and your gifts.

331

You are aligned with intelligence and divine love that will support you when required. Trust.

332

Your relationships are moving into a space of growth in order for you to feel content.

333

You are powerfully aligned with Jesus and other ascended masters at this time. You are at a crucial point on your journey where you can go beyond all previous setbacks.

334

Your guides and angels are circling around you, offering divine love and protection.

335

Change is only challenging when you forget that you are one with God and angels. Remember who you are.

336

Your heart requires your attention. Breathe and slow down to connect with your center before proceeding further.

337

You are in a portal of manifestation. Miracles are pouring from you at this time.

338

Your past lives hold the answers to the questions you are asking.

339

You are aligned with goddesses and powerful female saints who are helping you open up and welcome in divine love.

340

Your angels are helping you enter into a personal relationship with God. Know you are worthy of it.

341

Your expanding mind is opening you up to direct guidance from angels.

342

Your angel team want you to know they are guiding your relationships and addressing any concerns you have at this time.

343

Trust in the connections you feel within you—certain guides are communicating to and through you.

344

You are aligned with your guardian angel. They love you unconditionally.

345

Archangel Michael and his angels of protection are putting a ring of light and safety around you.

346

Trust that the angels you pray to are always guiding you to the perfect solution for you to grow.

347

Your higher self is manifesting opportunities that will push you beyond your comfort zone. Go beyond fear and grow.

348

Be open with the universe about what you really need to feel supported.

349

You don't need permission to be who you are. You were born to be powerful. Accept it.

350

Your guides are aligning your life with the power and light of abundance.

351

Don't fear the energy of change. It is always working according to the divine order and for your highest good.

352

Input in your relationships will be worth the effort. You are doing the right thing.

353

Your guides are encouraging you to move beyond your limitations and take time to face what you need to change in order to grow personally and spiritually.

354

Your angels are supporting you as you make your way through the shifts that are occurring at this time. Stay focused on the light and never let anything dull your sparkle.

355

Ascended masters are encouraging you to bring light and love into all your transactions regarding finance and abundance. Align your practices with the light.

356

This is a time of expansion and it's important for you to connect with how you are serving others. This will open up the channels for God to serve you.

357

Open your mind to seeing things differently. You are being encouraged to prepare for the miraculous, and as you change your perception, you will experience a miraculous shift.

358

It's important to have intentions, but also to be open to events not quite going to plan. Know that God's plan is always working in your favor.

359

Your angels want you to connect deeply with yourself and recognize that you are the brightest and the lightest you have ever been. Well done on all your inner work.

360

In order for you to experience harmony, God is inviting you to take an inventory of what is best serving you at this time and then proceed accordingly.

361

Your soul is asking you to reconnect with your initial intentions before proceeding further. You are being diverted from what will serve you. Get back on track.

362

Your relationships require your presence at this time and it's important to be open to feedback that is coming your way. Remember, every relationship you have is an assignment.

363

Your heart is expanding and you are opening up your spiritual senses. It's important to make sure you are calling in support and protection from the divine to sustain your expansion.

364

Your angels are with you. Call on their help and support and move forward with confidence, knowing you are being guided.

365

You have an opportunity for increased abundance at this time. Your angels are encouraging you to reconnect with your divine worth.

366

Stop. Do not go any further until you have reconnected with your intentions and sought expert information. This situation could stand in the way of your growth.

367

Whatever blockages you may have experienced are now being cleared from your energy. Things are beginning to move forward.

368

Your pathway and purpose are unfolding just as they need to. Know that your soul will always tell you what will serve your joy and contentment.

369

You may feel sensitive at this time, but it's important to listen in, as the emotions rising up in you are messages about what's most important for your journey going forward.

370

God and ascended masters are helping you manifest your intentions at this time. Focus on high energy and gratitude and you will usher in miracles.

371

Your intentions have been noted. Trust that the outcome is unfolding as it needs to.

372

Angel guidance is reminding you to bring those who matter most to you into your future visions and intentions. Share your abundant thinking.

373

Your higher self is manifesting important lessons so that you can step into a teacher/leadership role in your current situation. Take time to read between the lines of what's happening.

374

Your angels approve of your current intentions. Know that you are being encouraged to take the steps to make them reality.

375

You are being reminded to feel comfortable with change. The key is remembering that God and your angels are always with you.

376

When fear rises up, know that you are on the verge of something miraculous. Trust and call in support.

377

The miracle that you are seeking is within your grasp. Stay focused and aligned with the power and the light of love.

378

Your next step has been delivered, but you must proceed before knowing what happens next. Move forward.

379

Reconnect with your power. Remember who you are and what gifts you have. Know you were born to shine.

380

God wants you to know that you are powerful and you can do this.

381

Your angels are guiding you and your current situation will soon make sense. Know you are aligned with strength.

382

You are being connected and reconnected with friends and other relationships that are important for your growth. Open your mind.

383

You are being encouraged to drop your guard and take peaceful action at this time.

384

You are an Earth angel and you are being encouraged to find joy and contentment through service. Be willing to help others.

385

You are being encouraged to know that there are many ways forward. Let go of any stubbornness and be willing to see your current situation differently.

386

Taking the time to review your situation before continuing isn't giving up, it's preparing for a more enlightening and supportive experience.

387

You are being directed toward the truth, the answer, and the light. Trust what you see, hear, and feel.

388

Your way forward is now being revealed. Trust that divine guidance is there for you.

389

The road you are on is simply leading you back to yourself. You are the wise teacher. Go within and listen.

390

God is grateful to you.

391

Your commitment to growth is recognized throughout the cosmos. Thank you for your dedication to the light.

392

You are surrounded by positive and powerful people. Soak up the goodness and share it with your tribe.

393

There is powerful information within you that is ready to be heard. Your soul is encouraging you to listen through mindfulness, meditation, and journaling.

394

Your angels are inviting you to see yourself in a loving way. Love yourself.

395

The universe needs you to surrender your concerns so that it can support you. Let go and let God.

396

You are being encouraged to go within before you move forward. Remember who you are.

397

Your experiences are reflections of the energy that you are aligning with. Let yourself connect with what lights you up.

398

Your angels are reminding you to take the high road. Don't let anything throw you off path, especially when you have come this far.

399

You have downloaded powerful and insightful messages from the divine. Watch for them being revealed to you in meditations, visions, and dreams.

400

You are in direct communication with God. Know that your prayers are heard.

401

Let yourself be sustained by the love and presence of God. You are not alone.

402

Your guides and angel team are helping you with your current situation. Be the angel in your relationships.

403

Your energy is going through an upgrade at this time. Know that your guides are supporting you during this transition.

404

God and angels are putting a sacred light of protection around you. You are safe.

405

The changes that are occurring are God-led. Trust that the unfolding of your path is divinely directed.

406

You are being invited to pause and go within because God and angels have already placed the answers you need within you.

407

You are in a high-vibrational space at this time and are encouraged to focus on what you are ready to manifest.

408

You are here to live with a higher purpose. It will align when you do what sparks your joy.

409

Your higher self is always connected to God and angels. Know that you can connect with divine intelligence at all times.

410

You are being reminded to be clear about your intentions. God is always listening and will respond if your will aligns with divine law.

411

You are aligned with the oneness of life. All the support and guidance you need is with you now. Listen. Carefully.

412

It's important for you to be clear about your feelings and intentions at this time, particularly with regard to relationships.

413

Angels are supporting you, but only you can take the next step. Take a leap.

414

Your angels are reminding you of their presence. Trust that the experiences that you are having are connections with the divine.

415

Your angels are encouraging you to make the changes you know you need to make in order to grow. Take back your power.

416

When you stop overthinking and overplanning and get out of your own way, your angels will be able to move in and provide miraculous support and solutions.

417

Your angels are encouraging you to see the magic behind your current situation. Know that nothing happens by accident.

418

Your angels are guiding you to see that your pathway has been a powerful teacher and previous lessons have messages for you now.

419

Your angels are encouraging you to take back your power. Don't allow yourself to be overlooked.

420

Your angels are helping you develop a personal bond with the divine. You are being encouraged not to let anyone's negative teachings about God get in your way.

421

Your angels are encouraging you to focus lovingly on your relationship with yourself.

422

You are being guided to offer a helping hand to those around you. Ask how you can be of service to those in need. Giving to others will reward you too.

423

Angels and ascended masters are supporting you in recovering lost gifts and lost aspects of yourself.

424

Your angels are focusing on your personal relationships. Be clear about your feelings and share the love you have within with those you really care for.

425

Your angels are encouraging you to connect with the lessons of your current situation.

426

You are being guided to surround yourself with those who lift you up and encourage your light to shine.

427

Your angels are supporting your prayers and requests about romance and relationships.

428

Your angels are hearing your prayers regarding career and purpose and want you to know that they support your dreams.

429

Your angels are encouraging you to connect with the tender aspects of yourself at this time. Your vulnerability is a gift.

430

Your angels are encouraging you to reconnect with the purpose behind your current choices and actions, as this will help you keep moving forward.

431

You are surrounded by a group of angels, saints, and masters who are encouraging you to stay focused and aligned with the light.

432

You are being encouraged to call in support and guidance with regard to your relationships and connections with others.

433

Angels and Jesus are reminding you that the connection to the kingdom of heaven is within you.

434

Angels are responsible for some of the changing energies around you at this time. It is a response to the prayers that you have been sending to them.

435

You are being guided to upgrade your thoughts, actions, and intentions. Be the angel everywhere you go.

436

It's important to take time to reconnect with your heart and what lights you up before making any more decisions.

437

Your angels are supporting you by manifesting miracles.

438

Angels are reminding you that the spiritual path is not always easy and urging you to stay focused on the purpose behind what you are doing.

439

Angels are encouraging you to connect with the divine feminine via prayer, meditation and going within.

440

Your angels are aligning you directly with God. Speak up and know you are being heard.

441

Your angels are reminding you that you are a powerful being. Call up your inner strength and send it out into the world.

442

Angels want you to know that they are guiding you in relationships and all matters of the heart.

443

Your angels are supporting you as your energy is being upgraded. New connections are being made at this time.

444

You are surrounded by 100,000 angels. Miracles are happening before your eyes.

445

The Archangels are guiding you. You are being filled with light, strength, and healing at this time.

446

Your angels are encouraging you to retreat in order to be revived. Balance is essential for your growth.

447

Your angels are connecting your prayers, intentions, and visions with opportunities that will support your expansion. Enjoy new ventures.

448

Your angels are encouraging you to know that they are creating and curating your path according to your intentions and divine law.

449

You are in touch with angels and the Divine Mother. Allow yourself to give and receive love.

450

God and Archangel Michael are supporting you as you face fears, challenges, and setbacks. Know you are safe.

451

You must be prepared to make changes in order for the miracles you need to be brought to you.

452

Angel wisdom is encouraging you to share the truth that you have been holding in your heart. Openness will allow divine guidance in.

453

Angels are encouraging you to be clear about your plans and intentions so that you can be guided and supported.

454

It's time to let go of the need to control your life and let angels guide you toward brilliance, support, and love.

455

Big changes are occurring at this time so that you can be more aligned with abundance and expansion.

456

Angels are encouraging you to align with the energy of care and compassion. Ignore any thoughts of attack.

457

Expressing your spiritual gifts will allow a wave of spiritual support into your life. Call on archangels for help in embracing your gifts.

458

Spiritual healing is surrounding you at this time to sustain you as you continue on your pathway of growth.

459

Your angels are encouraging you to prepare for miracles.

460

God is encouraging you to take extra care of yourself at this time, as it is crucial you are energized for the next phase of your journey.

461

Know that your internal vision of yourself can be healing. Continue to lovingly encourage yourself from within.

462

You are being encouraged to cut the cords between you and relationships that are not supporting you or making you feel whole.

463

Your angels are encouraging you to do all you can to love and care for your body. This will clear the road ahead.

464

Your angels are with you now. Welcome their help and rely on their support.

465

Your experience of miracles is down to your capacity to believe they are possible and you are worthy of them.

466

Your angels are encouraging you to gather more information before proceeding further.

467

Your angels are reminding you that you have the capacity to manifest miracles in your life. Believe in your magic.

468

Your angels are supporting you. Know that they are clearing lower vibrations from your energy and life.

469

You are in direct connection with an important aspect of what you have to learn. Be open to information rising up from within.

470

God and angels are helping you understand universal mysteries at this time.

471

Your angels are reminding you of your power to be a leader, teacher, and healer on the Earth. Know that your gifts were given to be shared.

472

Your gifts cannot be gifts unless you give them to others. You are being encouraged to share your talents with the world.

473

Your angels want you to know that forgiveness is an important lesson to learn before the next phase of your journey unfolds.

474

Your angels are supporting the manifestation of your dreams. Have unwavering faith.

475

With change and power comes great responsibility. You are being invited to stay grounded and connected with God as you move forward.

476

Your angels are guiding you to face your fears and ask yourself what they are teaching you. Know that the love within you can overcome anything.

477

You are connected to the energies and laws of manifestation at this time. Imagine that your prayers have already been answered in order to experience the reality.

478

Your angels are encouraging you to connect with the Earth. Get grounded in order to feel back on track.

479

Angel guidance is encouraging you to unleash your inner teacher in order to realign yourself with your highest good.

480

Nothing is happening by chance. Trust that the road ahead is leading to your highest good.

481

Angels are helping you reconnect with previous lessons so that you do not have to repeat old patterns.

482

Your angels are encouraging you to follow your path and do what is working for you, rather than making your dreams small to accommodate those of others.

483

You are here to grow, and this won't occur without mistakes. But your angels want you to know that you are loved no matter what. Surrender your guilt to God.

484

You are being encouraged to trust in the kingdom of heaven. Your angels are working on your behalf and are standing close to you now.

485

You are being reminded that you were born to love and be loved. Remove yourself from situations that do not support this truth.

486

Your angels are encouraging you to remember that "No!" *is* an answer. You should use it more often.

487

Your journey entails you being a teacher, leader, and spokesperson. Stand up and be heard.

488

Your angels are encouraging you to know that to teach is to learn. You are being encouraged to shine.

489

Your angels are waiting for you to arrive at the cave of your heart, so take time to go within. Love is waiting for you there.

490

You are aligned with your higher self and guided by God.

491

Angels are grateful for you and see you as a beacon of light.

492

Your angels are encouraging you to take time to breathe. Be cool, calm, and collected before you move forward.

493

You are being connected with your loved ones in heaven. Know that those you pray to regularly are protecting you just like guardian angels.

494

Your angels are encouraging you to express the real you. It's time to stop holding back from who you really are.

495

You are being encouraged to make the changes you know your soul needs in order to grow. You were born to feel bright and shiny.

496

Connect with what brings you closer to God and to love. Let go of all that is not serving you.

497

Your energy is opening up and new opportunities to experience harmony are being presented to you.

498

You are in a sacred space where you are increasing your self-awareness and connection with your truth. Know you are being guided along the path you are walking.

499

Your angels are directing you through your inner voice and intuition. Trust the information that is rising up within you at this time.

500

God is preparing the road ahead. Get ready to experience miracles and abundance.

501

Know that God is supporting all you do that is aligned with light and goodness.

502

Your relationships and connections with others are changing. Trust that God is helping you with these shifts.

503

Your growth at this time is down to your capacity to trust that God is always working for you and for the highest good of all.

504

Your angels are with you, guiding you to cultivate what's important and let go of what's not.

505

Trust in the changes you feel you are guided to make, as these are God-led. You have the capacity to manifest abundance. Believe it.

506

Your growth is dependent on how much joy you are allowing to flow through your body and life. Let joy become something you strive to experience and share.

507

You are being guided to make room for miracles. Miracles manifest when you clear the way for them.

508

Stay focused on what lights you up and brings you a sense of purpose. The rest of your road is being taken care of by God.

509

You are in touch with something important. Keep listening and allow God's messages to come through your heart.

510

Your hard work and dedication to growth are being recognized. Know that you are always connected to the divine and that experience of it is always personal.

511

Your determination to be a light to the world is making a difference in the hearts of those who need it most. Keep up the good work.

512

Take time to make peace in relationships where you have experienced challenges. Show that you are willing to move forward in a loving way.

513

Your efforts to expand and to experience a life of abundance are preparing the road ahead. Stay focused on how you can grow and let the light lead.

514

Your angels are encouraging you to continue applying yourself to the highest and best. Your life is an example to others of what is possible for them.

515

Change is what you make of it. See the changes happening now as opportunities to grow and be your most authentic self.

516

Taking time to assess what is allowing you to experience more joy and what is standing in the way of your light will enable you to know which way to move from here.

517

The shifts you are encountering in your energy are in relation to your current situation. You are being guided to cut the cords and let go. When you do, you will see the miracle and the solution that you need.

518

It's important to ask for what you need, rather than focusing on what you want. Let God give you what will sustain your wellness.

519

Your angel guidance is to relax and breathe. You don't need to fight to prove yourself or your power. Let your work speak for itself.

520

Your connection to God is stronger than ever. Welcome home to love.

521

What you are seeing in others is a reflection of what is also within you. Let go of the need to judge and see the world through loving eyes.

522

You are in a powerful space that is connected with the energy of forgiveness. Know that forgiveness is the remembering that you can never really be hurt, for nothing can tarnish your soul.

523

You are stepping forward and stepping up. Know that you are on the right path.

524

Angels are supporting you and your loved ones as you move into a more harmonious and serene state.

525

The energy of wellness, miracles, and hope is surrounding you, your loved ones and your relationships at this time. Embrace all that is meaningful to you.

526

You were born to be light, bright, and filled with joy. Take time to make sure your relationships are allowing you to be your best self.

527

Your current situation is a manifestation of unshared feelings. It's important for you to open up. In turn that will clear the way ahead.

528

Angels love and respect you, and invite you to continue working on loving and respecting yourself. They are overjoyed by your commitment to self-love.

529

You are experiencing changes that will improve your relationships with the important women in your life. Mother healing is possible at this time.

530

Jesus and God are leading you through the changes that you are facing. Trust them with all of your heart and never doubt your own innate wisdom.

531

The Keepers of the Light are blessing and supporting all of your current aims and commitments. Know that you are being encouraged to continue.

532

Your angels are encouraging you to surrender and trust in the strength of a higher power. You can be supported if you let the love in.

533

You are on the ladder to ascension and will soon be releasing all of the ties that bind you to fear and old feelings of persecution. Call on Jesus to help you.

534

Ascended masters and your angels and guides are here to support your current ventures with their light and love. This is a blessed road.

535

The foundation of your road to expansion is your willingness to make the effort. Angel guidance is encouraging you to get motivated and prepared for your journey.

536

Your angels are reminding you that opportunity is based on your willingness to share, to be seen, and to recognize your gifts.

537

Your soul's growth depends on your willingness to step forward and accept opportunities as they are brought to you.

538

The journey that you are on is forever expanding. Take time to see how far you have come and who you have become.

539

In order to move forward, you are being encouraged to reconnect to your lineage, and to the female figures in particular.

540

Angels have heard your prayers for change. Know that divine order is stepping in to support you as you move ahead.

541

You must make the changes that you are seeking. God will be with you as you take the steps, but you must take the first step.

542

You are being guided to be open and honest about what you need for your relationships to feel harmonious and safe. Speak up.

543

Your angels want you to know that they recognize your commitment to change and are guiding you toward growth and expansion.

544

Your angels are helping to make the changes necessary for you to feel safe and guided and to enjoy abundance. The doors to abundance will soon be opening.

545

Archangels, including Archangel Michael, are encouraging you to cut the cords to your current situation so that you can move back toward growth, expansion, and joy.

546

Archangels are inviting you to go within to reconnect with your heart and ask what will bring you closer to where you want to be and the energy you want to represent.

547

Angels are working on the prayers and intentions you have sent them. Know that the future is never set in stone and you'll be led toward what is of best service to you and the world.

548

Your career and purpose are in a state of flux at this time. Know that angels will always try to align your experiences with what lights you up.

549

Your angels are encouraging you to listen to the voice within and be prepared to make the changes it is asking for, as these are the steps you need to take to have a miraculous life.

550

God is giving you the answers to your prayers. Pay attention and be open-minded enough to think beyond your own expectations.

551

Within you there is a light, and that light will never go out. Remember who you are and trust that the light will guide you to where you need to be.

552

You are being invited to take light, joy, and peace into your home, your relationships and everywhere you go.

553

Your input and efforts are being acknowledged and will pay off. Continue with your current momentum.

554

There is a fine line between effort and effortlessness. Your angels are inviting you to trust them and their ability to help you. Believe.

555

All of your efforts are paying off. Abundance is yours to have, live, and experience. Open up your heart, arms, and mind to receive the blessings that are being offered to you now.

556

In order to receive, you must be prepared to give. Give gracefully, receive graciously. Your gifts are not gifts unless they are shared.

557

Your beliefs are manifesting the experiences you are having. Reconnect with your values and align yourself with abundance and plenty.

558

The road ahead is clearing and you are moving forward in a fearless way. Know that divine love is on your side.

559

Your true self and your physical self are forming a divine connection. Feel whole within and reap the benefits of wellness in your life.

560

Your angels are encouraging you to make a conscious effort to slow down. Commit to being more mindful and you will open yourself up to support.

561

Your current projects require your commitment and focus. Angel guidance is encouraging you to remove distractions and anything that could get in the way of your expansion.

562

In order for those around you to change, you must be willing to change old habits and patterns that could be blocking your growth. Remember, relationships are teachers to teachers.

563

The universe will be able to serve you better when you are willing to release the old stories that you are hanging on to. Release the need to be a victim and step into the space of being a co-creator.

564

Your angels are supporting you in being comfortable in your own skin and your own space, and are encouraging you to love yourself.

565

Any concerns about finances and investments, including overcoming financial setbacks, are now being eased. The answers you need are being delivered to you.

566

Angel guidance is encouraging you to step back and get more information before proceeding further. Don't make any sudden changes, as they could impact your recovery and growth.

567

Any concerns you have are now being ironed out and you are being encouraged to move forward rather than hold back. Miracles are being created for you today.

568

You are not being blocked or held back, you are just being encouraged to trust. You lack information only because the next phase of your journey won't be created until you make the next move. But know that the universe is on your side.

569

You have real self-awareness at this time. Your soul's voice is louder than ever and you are being encouraged to trust the messages that are rising up inside you!

570

God has heard your prayers and will answer your call for support soon.

571

The situation you are facing is an important lesson that will remind you of your innate power. Be willing to see your gifts and accept that you have been given them.

572

Taking time to connect with your higher self is important now. Your soul is ancient and has much experience that you can connect with and even remember.

573

Your thoughts of abundance and willingness to share are creating new ways forward that will allow you to feel guided and supported.

574

Your angels are encouraging you to take forward any ideas, business ventures, or opportunities to learn that you have felt drawn to. You are receiving divine guidance.

575

You are in a magical space. Prepare for the best possible outcome to your current situation, as the stars are aligned in your favor.

576

The next phase of your journey will start when you willingly face your fears. Know that you are not alone and you can do this.

577

Miraculous and magical situations are arising at this time. Embrace all the goodness that is unfolding.

578

Be willing to embrace the changes that are happening in your personal life. They will bring you a deeper sense of joy and fulfillment.

579

You are being invited to step into the leader and teacher role and lead by example. Your power and light are inspirational.

580

Know that the small changes you are making in your life are making a big difference to the world. God is grateful for your efforts.

581

Your angels are inviting you to review the setbacks you have overcome and amazing changes you have experienced on your journey so far. You are a miraculous being.

582

You are being reminded that relationships are journeys and offer powerful opportunities for you to know yourself more deeply.

583

Your angels are encouraging you to recognize the efforts that you are making. Approve of yourself and what you are doing, especially if you feel undervalued by others.

584

The angel of direction is with you now and is encouraging you to choose your pathway then take the steps that you know you need to take.

585

Your journey on Earth is to be enjoyed. Bring joy into all that you are doing and you will create roads to opportunity and abundance.

586

Angel wisdom is inviting you to bring light into all that you are doing. Remember that beings of light are with you at all times. Embrace their loving presence.

587

Your journey is manifesting opportunities for you to step up and stand in your power once more. This is a time for you to reclaim your voice and confidence.

588

Like a phoenix, you are in a powerful state of change and transition and rising high above what once held you back. Spread your wings and soar.

589

Your recent experiences have been powerful teachers and reminders that you are more in touch with yourself than you have previously given yourself credit for. Self-care is essential at this time.

590

God is grateful that you are finally back on the spiritual pathway. The diversion you took was necessary, though, as now you will appreciate who you are and who you have become.

591

Your life experiences are powerful teachers to the world. Your angels are encouraging you to stay focused on bringing your best to the world.

592

You are in touch with people who could be influential on your journey and powerfully supportive of your growth.

593

Your energy is being upgraded at this time. It's important to know that nothing is off, you are just being connected on a deep level.

594

Your angels are opening your crown chakra so that you can receive divine guidance. Soul memories are being uncovered.

595

Your chakras are being aligned with crystalline light, allowing you to open up to powerful information that will align you with a higher purpose.

596

Your spiritual muscles need time and space to recover. You are working hard on self-mastery, but this also requires space and time to play and have fun.

597

Your energy is magnetic at this time and is attracting powerful angels who are surrounding you with golden light and opportunities.

598

Your efforts to expand your gifts and offerings have been recognized. Doors, windows, and portals to opportunity are all being opened for you now.

599

You are in a space of deep knowing and connection. Trust the divine wisdom that is coming to you and moving though you.

600

God is restoring your energy at this time. Take time to breathe and feel replenished.

601

You are being guided to connect with your center. Take time to be honest and patient with yourself. This is a time for recuperation.

602

It's important to find time for friendships and relationships. You will benefit from seeing others and you have much to give and share.

603

You are experiencing a surge of psychic and spiritual awareness at this time. Know that your insights and visions are divinely inspired. Trust the messages you are hearing.

604

Your angels are adding loving energy to your energy. It's important to take time to feel topped up and replenished.

605

Your access to abundance isn't blocked, but you are being invited to get real about your intentions, as you have let yourself be sidetracked.

606

Bring your vision, goals, purpose, and finances into alignment with God and you will be sustained by the power and presence of love.

607

You are being brought into alignment with the magic and power of your soul. Feel ignited by the knowledge that you are connected to heaven and Earth.

608

You have an opportunity to make a change. Know that you are being given a chance to start a new venture and vision.

609

You are receiving an important soul download. Take some moments to be still and receive the messages that are coming to you from within. Past-life information and healing can be accessed now.

610

Your energy is being aligned with God's and your soul's purpose. You are doing the right thing and following the right path.

611

Your heart, soul, and life are expanding through the sacred awareness that you are connected and aligned with the life and light of all that is and ever will be.

612

Your heart requires you to be unreserved and honest in your relationships. Release the pressure that you are holding within.

613

Honesty with yourself is necessary for your expansion. It's important to check in with yourself and stop avoiding anything you have been putting off with regard to your wellness and self-care.

614

Your angels are encouraging you to reconnect with yourself and your needs before proceeding further. It's important for you to feel replenished with energy before you take on anything else.

615

Abundance is a natural expression of universal energy based upon your capacity to see your worth. Angel wisdom is encouraging you to dive deep within and realize you are deserving of abundance.

616

The universe is encouraging you to do what is best for your mental and emotional wellbeing. Make space for yourself.

617

The next door will not open for you until you close a door to the past. Angel wisdom is encouraging you to lovingly release all that is standing in the way of your joy and growth.

618

Your angels are encouraging you to connect with what brings you joy and pleasure before moving ahead. If you have to choose between joy and grief, you are being especially encouraged to choose joy.

619

You are being reminded that your power lies in your actions, "non-actions" and choices. Take control of your current situation so that you can direct its outcome.

620

You are overcoming disruptions to your personal spiritual connection. God is glad to have a relationship with you once more.

621

Your relationship with yourself has improved radically and you are in a miraculous space of self-respect now. Know that you deserve this.

622

Harmony and balance are being brought to your personal relationships at this time. All obstacles to love are being cleared.

623

There's a feeling of moving up and moving on around you. Any blocks to communication and understanding are being removed.

624

Your angel team is drawing close and encouraging you to do what you love. Now is the time for you to spread your wings and fly high.

625

Your angels are encouraging you to let go of the need to control events in your workplace or creative outlets at this time. When you take a step back, you allow the guidance of heaven in.

626

Your angels are guiding you to practice extreme self-care at this time. Move your body, do what brings you balance and make mental space for clarity.

627

Your angel guides are encouraging you to say "No" to opportunities you know will cause you pain and concern. Then you can say "Yes" to yourself and your growth.

628

Angel wisdom is reminding you that your function is to experience and express happiness. You are being guided to do what lights you up and sparks great joy in your heart.

629

Thank you for taking the time to gather your thoughts and energy and concentrate on your wellbeing. Your soul is now full of light and inspiration and your efforts will be rewarded.

630

Angels are reminding you that you don't always have to be on the frontline doing the hard work. Give yourself credit and realize that the changes you have made recently, both internally and with others, are pleasing God and supporting the divine plan.

631

You are in a cave of energy at this time and it's important for you to drop into your heart and listen to the information that is being revealed to you. Remember, divine love is always within you.

632

Your sense of alignment and balance will be restored when you are honest in your relationships. Surrender your need to people please and share your authentic truth.

633

Ascended masters are upgrading your energy system at this time. You are experiencing clarity and connection in your spiritual vision and spiritual gifts.

634

Your angels want to thank you for taking the time to balance your energy system, as this has strengthened your connection to heaven and the spiritual realms.

635

Your angels are guiding you through the energy of change at this time. Know that you are being encouraged to make the decisions you know are necessary to move closer to joy and express your gifts.

636

Welcome home to yourself. It seems you are finally in a loving space with yourself once more. Angels are dancing around you in celebration of your self-acceptance.

637

Know that your intentions and manifestation prayers are being noted and answered in the perfect time–space sequence for your soul and the highest good of the world. Your angels are encouraging you to trust and be patient.

638

The point of your journey on Earth is to expand your consciousness and come into alignment with higher purpose. In previous lives or previously on this current journey you have experienced a great disconnect from God and spirit. Now it's time to recreate and strengthen that bond.

639

You are being encouraged to take time to receive. Sometimes the greatest sense of connection comes from accepting the world as it is before moving forward.

640

God and angels are opening your heart and energy so that you can experience and express divine love. You are here to gift the world with your presence.

641

Don't underestimate your gifts. You have a special light and talent to bring to this world. Angels are with you and encouraging you.

642

Your angels are encouraging you to realize the answer you are seeking is actually in you. Stop searching outside and go within.

643

What is coming from within is right and correct. Angel wisdom is encouraging you to trust in the messages that have been rising up inside you and follow them.

644

Your angels are expanding your heart chakra so that you can experience a deeper love and connection with them and with the guides and ancestors who are there for you.

645

Archangel Michael and Archangel Raphael are with you now. Know that you are protected and surrounded by healing energy.

646

Angels are encouraging you to take time to breathe and contemplate where you are before proceeding further. You are reminded that carefulness and patience are qualities of spirit.

647

Your angels are encouraging you to move forward. Stop waiting for permission. Take matters into your own hands. You are on the cusp of a miraculous moment.

648

Your path is clearing rapidly. All challenges, roadblocks and concerns are being removed so that you can feel in alignment once more.

649

Your angels are encouraging you to honor the feelings that are coming up for you at this time. They are actually messages from your soul about its growth.

650

God is giving you the answers, the miracles and all that you need to be on track and in alignment with what lights up your spirit.

651

Archangels are reminding you of the power of your will. Reconnect with your inner strength. Know you have it. You have already overcome and created so much.

652

You are being encouraged to bring your peaceful self to your relationships, both with those you love and those who are challenging you. Know that you have it within you to be the angel everywhere you go.

653

You are expanding your energy and your gifts. Know that any setbacks or feelings of being stuck are just energetic recalibrations so that your vibration can rise higher.

654

Your angels are supporting you through any changes that are necessary at this time. Know that as you make room for the new in your life, you also make room for miracles.

655

You are manifesting powerful opportunities for support and abundance. The love you have shared with the Earth is now washing back and blessing your life.

656

In the past, you have made many sacrifices with regard to your wellbeing. Now you are being encouraged to know that you no longer have to do this. It's time to live a more love-based story.

657

Your heart has endured many lessons with regard to love. Angel wisdom is reminding you that you are not here to search for love, you are here to remember that love is within, and in finding it there you will manifest it in your outer world.

658

Your energy is manifesting many roads to opportunity and joy. Know that there is never a wrong choice; every move you make brings you closer to purpose and fulfillment.

659

Know that your energy is expanding and your awareness of all things spiritual is increasing. Your recent actions and choices have been aligned with love. Your inner teacher is speaking loud and clear.

660

God is encouraging you to think things through before proceeding further.

661

God wants you to know that you are not being condemned and are already forgiven. Now forgive yourself.

662

The lessons you are experiencing are being presented because you are still lacking in understanding and forgiveness of other parties. Forgiving others is a gift of freedom to yourself.

663

Your energy requires your honest focus and attention at this time. It's important to follow the path that will take you to joy rather than your ego's wishes and false promises.

664

Angel wisdom is encouraging you to listen to the voice of your soul with regard to those you are choosing to surround yourself with at this time.

665

You are being encouraged to make the changes you know you need to make, as failure to do so will result in challenges that will hold you back from your highest good and freedom.

666

Halt. Stop. *No*. Do not make any sudden decisions. Your ego has taken control and is leading the way to heartache and fear. But you can recover your power. Call in the light of God.

667

You are now moving out of this challenging spell of despair and fear. Know that angels are guiding you. Have faith in yourself, your light, and your gifts.

668

Continue with your acts of kindness and self-care—they are lighting up the path ahead. Things will become lighter and easier from here.

669

Know that the worst of this situation is behind you. You are now returning to your true self and will feel energized, encouraged, and directed from here on.

670

God is surrounding you with power and light at this time. Stay focused on the best possible outcome of your situation and it will be manifested. Have faith.

671

The energy of hope is surrounding you at this time. Trust that your prayers are being heard and answered. The solution that you need is within your grasp and is being revealed to you now.

672

Your thoughts and intentions are directing the flow of life around you. Know that your relationships require some of your loving presence and attention in order for you to grow.

673

Your spirit has created a wave of grace that is clearing and lighting up your path. Your journey to manifesting miracles is unfolding perfectly.

674

Your angels want to be part of your bigger picture, but they need your permission. Call them in and allow them to support the expansion of your purpose and soul.

675

The changes you have made and are willing to make have been recognized by God and your angels. Know that your next steps are being revealed to you now. There is hard work ahead, but with dedication you can reach your goals.

676

You have an opportunity to feel realigned and more connected to your life purpose at this time. Angel wisdom is encouraging you not to give up on projects that previously lit you up more than they do now. Sort out any unfinished business.

677

What you are looking for is now being delivered to you. Miracles are entering your life and your prayers are being answered. Embrace the blessings.

678

There are opportunities on the horizon for you to grow both in yourself and your career. Step into focused mode and prepare for an exciting road ahead. You are moving up a rung on the ladder to success.

679

Your higher self and internal wisdom are in alignment with the opportunities that are being presented to you at this time. Angel guidance is encouraging you to take a leap of faith, knowing that you are being supported.

680

God is supportive of your current focus and choices, and your path is being blessed by the power and presence of love. Enjoy the support.

681

Take time to understand some of the messages, patterns, and lessons that are being revealed to you at this time. Remember that your thoughts and intentions play a part in your experiences.

682

Your angels are encouraging you to remember that the journey you are on is *your* journey. Stop relying on others or waiting for them to come with you, as you will be waiting a while and this is *your* dream. So, trust in your own abilities and talents.

683

You are being encouraged to give yourself love and understanding with regard to any mistakes you may have made or setbacks you may have contributed to in the past. You did the best you could. Now let go of these old stories and write a new one.

684

It's important for you to begin revealing your talents and allowing them to become a powerful part of your future. Your angels are supporting you.

685

Change isn't bad, it's a blessing. Angel wisdom is encouraging you to know that you will experience many changes on your path. Trust that the best way forward will always be revealed to you.

686

The lesson that you are learning at this time isn't a setback, but an opportunity for you to clear your path. It's important to do everything within your power to resolve the current situation, though, before proceeding further.

687

Your angels are encouraging you to step into a teacher/leader position in your current situation. The messages and lessons you can share with others are also ones that you need to hear.

688

Your path is blessed by God and angels. Golden opportunities are coming your way. Expect miracles.

689

Welcome back to the cave of your heart. You are back in touch with your true self. And love is who you are.

690

God is proud of who you have become. Thank you for believing in yourself once more.

691

Your commitment to growth and to your soul is being recognized. This commitment is important, because the better you know yourself, the better you will know God and your angels.

692

There are opportunities for you to experience a new sense of love, either in a new relationship or via the rekindling of a current connection. Either way, know that this is a time for love.

693

Your capacity to love and be loved is based on your capacity to know you are deserving of love. You *are* deserving. Love is yours. Love is your inheritance.

694

Your angels are grateful that you are taking time to regularly connect with them and receive their messages. If a message is coming from within right now, know that it is angelically inspired.

695

The universe is mapping out your path according to your level of awareness and commitment to growth. Know that you will never be handed anything you cannot handle. Reconnect with your will and its incredible power to make the impossible possible.

696

Your angels are encouraging you to trust in the flow of life, particularly if you feel as though things have slowed down recently. Surrender your constant need to be busy and remember that less is more.

697

Your dreams, aspirations, and goals are manifesting rapidly at this time, due to your commitment to expansion and self-worth. Enjoy the blessings and know that they are reminders that you are a powerful, beautiful, and deserving soul.

698

Your journey is beginning to speed up and the steps you have been searching for are being presented to you. Thank you for trusting in the divine plan.

699

Your inner Buddha is being activated now. Trust any enlightened thoughts or visions that you are having, for they are being inspired by your soul's memories.

700

Know that God is behind you and with you every step of the way. The miracle you need is already within you. Trust in your power to light up the world.

701

The intention and manifestation energy around you is powerful at this time. Stay focused on the path.

702

God is helping you with your relationships. Know that there are opportunities for you to grow closer to your loved ones at this time.

703

Know that your vision for the future is rapidly unfolding before your eyes. Divine wisdom is encouraging you to stay motivated and focused on the best outcome.

704

Your angels' presence and messages are physically manifesting around you. Open your eyes and mind to seeing things differently and be aware of your angels supporting you.

705

You are drawing down the energy of the stars at this time and being encouraged to set your sights higher than you have previously.

706

Your ability to manifest miracles will be unlocked when you clear the emotionally draining situations from your life. Take the power back into your own hands.

707

God has heard your prayers and wants you to know that the miracles you need to be in alignment with your highest goodness and truth are coming your way now. Enjoy the magic.

708

You are the keeper of your body and your life. Angel wisdom is reminding you not to fall victim to circumstances and to align your thoughts, intentions and actions with energy that is going to support you going forward.

709

The experiences that you are having at this time have been created by your soul and support your soul's growth. Open your heart to new opportunities and new ways forward.

710

The power of God is within you. Spiritual experiences are unfolding for you and supporting your expansion in the world.

711

The universe is behind your endeavors and adventures. The power of oneness is entering your heart and helping you to bring radical changes to your life. In turn these changes will lovingly support the growth and healing of the world.

712

Your relationships with those who are close to you are important. Remember to bring light to your current connections and relationships and workplace. The lessons you are learning and teaching must begin in your own life.

713

There is a feeling of moving up and moving forward around you at this time. Small synchronicities will lead on to greater miracles. Your faith is paying off and your angels are inviting you to stay aligned with this positivity.

714

Your angels are willing to support you on your journey going forward and are reminding you that you don't have to work out every detail in advance. Call in all the help you need and you will find the way ahead being revealed to you.

715

Your angels are congratulating you on your recent manifestations and miracles. All that you are experiencing now is a reminder that you are connected to the creative force of the universe.

716

Your angels are helping you feel rejuvenated and connected at this time. This energy of replenishment is required as your next steps will require focus and dedication. This is the calm before the storm.

717

Your magic is being unlocked. You are in a magical portal which will allow you to manifest your dreams. Stay in alignment with your highest thoughts and feelings in order to usher in big magical changes.

718

Taking time to focus on your blessings and the miracles you have experienced on your path this far will hold you in a magnetic space to create even more. This is a time to be blessed, and it starts with seeing the love that is already present in your life.

719

Don't be afraid of your power. You are connected to and charged by the cosmic powers of the universe. God is with and within you, and reminding you that sharing your gifts is not to be feared but celebrated.

720

The watchful eyes of God and angels are on your life and your relationships at this time. It's important for you to set goals and aspirations with your loved ones so that they can feel honored and part of your bigger picture.

721

You are establishing your personal relationship with the universe at this time. Previously you may have felt disconnected from the divine, but now you really know that you are loved.

722

You are at a crucial point of your journey. Remember that you are worthy of being helped, as focusing on that worthiness is going to bring radical opportunities for you to be seen and heard. Call in the angels of manifestation, as they are willing to help you.

723

There is an energy of moving up and moving forward around you at this time, but it's important to release the need to measure your success and to focus more on the blessings you can bring to the Earth. Small steps are still steps. Know that angels are with you!

724

This is a time for you to honor and be honored. Know that when angels look at you, they see a spark of greatness and love.

725

Angel wisdom is encouraging you to unleash your spirit at this time. Don't hold back—reveal your untamed wild self and dance to the sacred rhythm of life.

726

Your journey will be much smoother when you review those you surround yourself with and let into your inner circle. Ask for guidance and follow your intuition about who can be trusted.

727

You are the magician. You are the priest(ess). You are the connector of the realms. The power and presence of heaven are with and within you now.

728

You are being presented with an opportunity to make subtle changes to your path so that you are more in alignment with your initial intentions. Reconnect with your initial wishes, then evaluate what is happening now and make any necessary changes.

729

You are being reminded that trust in God and in spirit is essential if you wish to see the way ahead. Let go of your need to question and have faith.

730

Your current experiences are showing those around you what is also possible for them. It's important for you to stay graceful and grounded, as this will keep the wave of blessings flowing into your life.

731

Ascended masters are blessing your road to self-mastery with their light. So, move into your true self and rise above darkness. Light is within you.

732

Angel wisdom is encouraging you to forgive in order to heal. See the light in all and remember that when you are connected to love there is nowhere your love cannot go.

733

Jesus and the Holy Spirit are blessing you with their light. Spirit has your back and miracles are following on naturally from your expression of love. Know that love is real.

734

Your angel team is revealing truths, including an understanding of your current situation, through energetic downloads. Take time to unlock these deep insights from heaven and the astral realm.

735

This is a time for you to experience infinite abundance. Obstacles are now being removed from your pathway and spiritual support is increasing. It's important to embrace all the changes as they are presented to you.

736

You are being guided to upgrade your personal psychic protection methods. It's important to care for your energy and your emotional wellbeing. Cut the cords connecting you to the past and call on the supreme protection of heaven.

737

Angels are encouraging you to stay calm and centered at this time. Trust in the goodness in yourself and in others. Stay focused on the light, and as you connect with it you will create blessings and turn your dreams into reality.

738

You are being guided to trust in heaven and know you are safe. Angels are always with you and are standing close at this time. Surrender any concerns you have about your pathway to heaven and you will allow that pathway to unfold.

739

Your heart is awakening at this time and the masters of the divine feminine are encouraging you to welcome in divine love. An important lesson about giving and receiving in balance is unfolding for you.

740

God and angels are encouraging you to connect with the Earth at this time. As you get grounded, you will uncover important information about your journey.

741

Your angels are helping you see yourself through their loving eyes. You have conquered many old fears and overcome setbacks regarding your self-worth. Your newfound self-respect will carve out opportunities for you to stand in service and be served while you serve.

742

Your angels are encouraging you to trust that higher learning is being revealed at this time. It's important for you to see that your previous experiences have been great teachers. More inner study is now required to progress.

743

This is a time for you to rediscover aspects of yourself and your gifts that have been hidden and forgotten. Your guardian angels are drawing close and helping you dive deep within and see yourself through the eyes of excitement and wonder.

744

Angels are blessing your pathway with spiritual abundance. All of your previous concerns about security, wellness, or having enough are now being overcome. The doors to opportunity are being opened and your income is increasing.

745

Archangel Michael is helping you feel safe as you become your true self. Don't hold back—this isn't a time to be afraid. Rather, it is a time for you to celebrate who you are. Know that angels are celebrating with you—celebrating your deep inner self-acceptance.

746

Angel wisdom is encouraging you to get motivated and get moving. This isn't a time to hold back, this is a time to move forward. Don't let your ego run the show, let your spirit and your angel team light up the way.

747

This is a time for you to fly high. So, spread your wings and express everything you need to express in order to be free. Angels are flying with you and want to be part of your bigger picture.

748

You are receiving blessings at this time. You have made peace with many aspects of your past and this noble way of being is igniting your spirit and creating ways for you to raise your vibration and move closer to ascension.

749

Angel wisdom is encouraging you to take a leap of faith. It's important for you to know that you have powerful opportunities to learn, and the trust you have within will lead to a deeper connection with yourself.

750

God is granting your wishes and providing revealing answers to your prayers. You no longer need to ask; just take time to receive.

751

The lessons that you are being presented with are self-created. Angel wisdom is encouraging you to step into a space of self-love and self-acceptance, as this will clear any roadblocks and light up the answers you need to move forward in your mind.

752

The relationships in your life are powerful lessons for you. Take time now to get a weight off your chest. Speak up with love and make sure you are heard. Let angels help you.

753

You are releasing old lessons and karma at this time. Choose to move beyond drama and the drama of others. This is a time for you to create and curate your own path. Make room for positive energy and experiences.

754

Your angels are encouraging you to make the changes you need to receive divine order in your life. Do what you feel is right. An important lesson is unfolding.

755

A stargate is open and you are in a cosmic gateway of opportunity. Your thoughts are magnetic and powerful. The changes that are occurring now are in perfect alignment with your will and with divine order.

756

Angel wisdom is encouraging you to think about what you desire and set your sights high. Expect the best possible outcome and your focused intention will manifest a powerful reality for you.

757

Your consciousness is expanding as a result of your dedication to live your best life. Your soul is expanding too, and you are now beginning to understand your connection to all things and the lessons that your life is presenting you with at this time.

758

You are here to walk a pathway of truth. It's time to stand strong. Focusing on your purpose will help you feel supported. Release old fears regarding persecution and speak your truth. This will open up opportunities for you to move forward.

759

Divine alchemy—you are taking old energy that is like lead and turning it golden. You are moving beyond old stories and challenges and into a place of power and positivity.

760

God is encouraging you to listen to your angels' reminders to slow down. This is a time to be calm and mindful of all of your actions. Make sure you are aligning with truth and also taking into consideration all those around you and all those connected to your decisions.

761

Your angels are encouraging you to turn your attention to yourself before taking the next step. They will be happy to light up the road ahead, but first you must be honest with yourself.

762

Your devotion and care for those in your life has been recognized by heaven. You are being thanked for all of the sacrifices you have made in your life in service of others. Now it's time for *your* will and dreams to be served.

763

You are being aligned with your life-force at this time. Express your passions and don't be concerned about any powerful sexual energy that is rising up within you—this is the fire of your creative self igniting.

764

Your angels are encouraging you to spend time replenishing the energy within your aura and chakra system at this time. You may be feeling depleted, but don't let this get you down or hold you back. Just take time to recover your energy before you move forward in a loving way.

765

Your finances and sense of security are being upgraded by angels. Prepare yourself for pleasant news that will support your experience of abundance.

766

Angels and ascended masters are encouraging you to shine your light more brightly than ever. Don't allow anyone or anything to get in the way of the light that you were born to shine. Internal guidance is coming through for you now. Listen!

767

This is a time for you to trust and thrive. Your gifts are being expressed and the angels around you are impressed by your capacity to shine brightly. Know that some of the best lessons come from being the teacher—it's time to share your knowledge with the world.

768

Angels are encouraging you to open up your heart and mind to new possibilities. There are many roads to happiness and light. Healing and supportive information are being revealed to you at this time. Expand your horizons.

769

Connect with your emotions in order to ignite your passions. Powerful manifestations will take place when you connect with the wild, raw, and untamed aspects of your being. It's time to reveal all of the elements of your true nature.

770

God is saying "Yes." Go. Move forward. Take action.

771

It's time to be honest about and track down what you really want, as you have made space for miracles to manifest. All that is needed now is your clarity.

772

Bring the whole of yourself to your relationships. You need to be present and open at this time. Relationships are about giving and receiving, and your angels want you to be less distracted and more present for the meaningful experiences of your life.

773

Any blockages that you are experiencing at this time are merely your own concerns and fears. Don't be afraid of your power and light, be brave and honest and take control. Warrior mode activated!

774

Your angels are helping you recognize the priorities in your life. This is a time for you to shed old skin and leave behind what has been draining your light and soul.

775

The direction angels are surrounding you at this time to help you make sense of the way ahead. They are waiting for you to be focused so that they can take you forward. Get focused and be open to guidance.

776

Angels are encouraging you to be patient a little longer, but want you to know that you are on the verge of the miracle you have been searching for. Breathe.

777

Your magic and manifesting abilities are increasing at this time. Tap into your inner superpowers and release your magic into the world.

778

Your angels are encouraging you to see beyond the current situation and trust that everything has a purpose. Know that everything is happening as it needs to in order for you to be aligned with goodness and truth.

779

The angels of love are surrounding you at this time and guiding you to open your heart. This is a time for you to love and be loved. Let love in and let love out!

780

Your current journey and lesson are about your lineage. God is reminding you that there is a reason behind your family experience and calling on you to face a family concern or wound so that an old pattern can be healed.

781

Angel wisdom is inviting you to recognize your own contribution to the path that you are on. The experiences that you are having wouldn't be the same without you, and it's important you recognize the light and talents you are bringing to the world.

782

Your current connection or relationship is a valuable experience for you. It's important to take the next step in it now, as this will give you a deeper, more visceral experience of love.

783

Your setbacks are not setbacks, they are opportunities for you to recognize your capacity to rise above darkness and challenge. Your light and capacity to recover are stronger and brighter than ever at this time.

784

Your angels are helping you understand the direction that you are currently moving in. Trust that all will be revealed when the time is right. Continue expressing your creativity and gifts in the meantime.

785

Angel wisdom is reminding you that you were born to live fully and with joy. Take time to eliminate all that is blocking your joy and focus on what is bringing you happiness.

786

Angels are reminding you of the power of the word "No." When you say "No" to energies that are draining and challenging, you clear space in your schedule for the manifestation of miracles.

787

Your energy is moving through a powerful upgrade so that you can be a greater catalyst of change and healing upon the Earth. The universe needs you and your gifts and is grateful you are ready to move forward with them.

788

The synchronicities that are occurring at this time are a reflection of the magnetic power you hold within your heart. You can make anything happen, so connect with your heart's deepest wishes, and if they are in service to your expansion, they will come true immediately.

789

Major spiritual changes are unfolding around you. This is a time for you to fully overcome your greatest fear and face darkness eye to eye. You have the chance to soar, but it's dependent on your willingness to overcome your darkest shadow.

790

Your inner strength is being ignited at this time. Move back to wholeness, knowing that God is sustaining you and supporting your path. Remember that all the power that you are seeking is within you, as is the kingdom of heaven.

791

Your life is coming into alignment with the divine plan. Trust that everything is unfolding exactly as it needs to.

792

You are being invited to rise up and honor the force within you. The universe is supporting you by presenting you with the steps to transcendence. Trust what is being given to you and move forward.

793

Your goals and aspirations require more time, patience, energy and commitment to manifest. Take more time for prayer, meditation, and spiritual connection and you will reap the benefits.

794

The signs and messages you are receiving are your angels reminding you of their loving presence. You never walk this path alone.

795

You are being given powerful psychic insights regarding your next step. The universe knows exactly what you need to be in alignment with your highest good.

796

Your angels are encouraging you to take one step at a time. Replenish your energy by connecting with nature and breathing some fresh air before moving forward.

797

Trust the emotions that are rising up within you at this time—they are helping you understand what is most important for you and your path.

798

Are you wondering if you are doing the right thing or on the right path? Release these concerns, as they are just your ego trying to hold you up. You are living with light and purpose, and angels are grateful to you.

799

Know you are connected to spirit. Your mediumship and spiritual connections are strengthening rapidly at this time.

800

You are being called to live a life of purpose. God wants to be a greater part of your life. If you are ready to take the next step, make your intentions clear and that step will be presented to you.

801

Angel guidance is encouraging you to stay focused on your own path and release your concerns about other people.

802

Your path will clear when you take time to assess how you can be more present in your relationships.

803

The opportunities that you have recently taken are important and will serve your spiritual growth.

804

Your angels are encouraging you to remember that your greatest gifts to the world are your truth and your willingness to share authenticity.

805

Your vulnerability is working in your favor. Trust in God and your angels and know that your path is unfolding beautifully.

806

Step into a state of mindfulness and tread carefully as you move forward upon your path. Gentleness is the key to self-connection at this time.

807

Your expression of excitement and joy is weaving wonder and miracles into your everyday life. Embrace them wholeheartedly.

808

You are in a position of strength. Trust that all is in order and remain focused on your truth.

809

Your journey isn't always about how far you have come, it's also about how deeply you have connected. Congratulations on dedicating time to yourself.

810

God is supporting you on your journey to a sense of connectedness and purpose.

811

Your path is opening up. Everything is in perfect alignment for your dreams to become reality.

812

The lesson you are experiencing at this time is because a relationship, or wound connected to a relationship, has not yet been dealt with. To avoid unnecessary challenges, it's important to connect with this before moving forward.

813

Express who you are, express your joy and all that lights you up, and the universe will support you.

814

Your angels will be a bigger part of your journey moving forward. Know that there is a higher purpose in you sharing angel light with the world.

815

Angels are sharing opportunities for new beginnings with you at this time. Remember that you always have a choice and are encouraged to choose the path that speaks to you.

816

You are being encouraged to take peaceful action at this time. See the current situation from the other person's point of view before moving forward. There's a lesson there.

817

Experiences and opportunities connecting you to a higher purpose are unfolding. Prepare yourself for greatness and blessings.

818

Angel guidance is encouraging you to be clear in your heart about how you want your current situation to unfold before you take any further action.

819

Angel guidance is encouraging you to ask yourself what will bring you closest to joy before you make any further decisions.

820

Your way forward is dependent on your capacity to trust in God's plan and surrender any of your own small thoughts that could get in the way of your greatness.

821

You are being guided to spend some time journeying and dreaming so that you can clear any thoughts or intentions that could get in the way of your light.

822

You are in a space where you could light up the world of someone around you. Remember that there's a light inside you and it's infectious. Bring your whole self to your friendships and relationships today.

823

Your current situation is moving toward a resolution. Know that angels and ascended masters are guiding you toward a higher purpose.

824

Your angels are shining a harmonious light on your current situation. Know that peace and serenity are close.

825

Your angels are glad that you have been willing to release emotionally draining situations from your past. Your road ahead is clear.

826

Take time to connect deeply with those you love and those who love you, so that you can reignite your light. You deserve to be cherished.

827

Trust that the signs you are receiving are messages that you are indeed on the right path and that God is supportive of your journey.

828

Your angels are dancing in celebration of all your personal and professional achievements. Take time to acknowledge your hard work.

829

The next step on your journey involves you connecting to the voices and messages of the powerful female saints, deities, and masters of the past. They are with you now. Be their voice in the world.

830

Your experiences have all been for a reason. Angel guidance is encouraging you to trust in your power, purpose, and path. You have an essential role to play in the world.

831

Ascended masters are encouraging you to dial in and connect with them at this time, as they have powerful downloads of information that will increase your awareness and understanding.

832

You are being encouraged to make time to connect to your own self, as that will help you connect to God's plan.

833

Jesus is with you and wants you to know that he is guiding you. You have light within you that can overcome all the shadows that you face.

834

Your angels are nurturing and protecting you on your journey of expansion.

835

Embrace change and know that all that is occurring is in alignment with divine law.

836

Your angels are encouraging you to make space for laughter and happiness. Release the serious energy that you have been focusing on, as it is dampening your light and your gifts.

837

What you have been praying for and working on internally is now being brought to you through your experiences. Trust that the universe is directing you to the best possible outcome.

838

Your current experiences are echoes of past lives and past experiences in this lifetime. Open up your awareness so you can understand the messages and the patterns or wounds that can be healed at this time.

839

You are uniting with the divine feminine and are being guided to open your heart and mind to divine intervention.

840

The road ahead is not all yours to figure out. Trust in God and your angels, as they are leading you to joy and growth.

841

Recognition and reclamation of your gifts are important at this time. When you remember who you really are, the road ahead will be paved for you.

842

Take time to acknowledge the gifts and talents of your loved ones—they need your light and positivity at this time.

843

Your angels are encouraging you to see through the eyes of your soul. See your life being filled with wonder and opportunity, and experience the reality.

844

Your angels need your permission in order to intervene and provide guidance at this time. Call in their help and support if you are ready to be led to the next step.

845

Archangel Michael is on standby, ready to help you remove any negativity and blockages from your life in a safe and loving way. Call on him now.

846

Your angels are encouraging you to be aware of your own body and energy at this time. Self-awareness is key to increasing self-worth and connection.

847

Your current experiences are manifestations of past actions and intentions. Angel guidance is encouraging you to clear old sarcastic thoughts about yourself and your gifts from your mind so that you can cultivate experiences that lift you up to joy.

848

Your purpose is expanding at this time. All the steps that you have been taking are being supported by heaven. You are doing the right thing.

849

Your angels are encouraging you to continue connecting with your emotions and uncovering any feelings you are still hanging on to from the past. Letting them go will create a clear view of what lies ahead.

850

Your journey is being accelerated by the spiritual laws of abundance at this time. Prepare yourself for miraculous moments.

851

Your path to success will unfold effortlessly when you remember your gifts and trust that all that you need is already within you.

852

You may be experiencing some difficulties or challenges in conversations or relationships right now, but resolving these matters is essential if you are to grow and experience more joy.

853

The universe is inviting you to trust in the divine plan. Trust that the unfolding of your journey is always for the highest good and truth.

854

The more you trust and the more you surrender, the more room you make for joy to enter your heart. Have faith now.

855

You are rapidly manifesting opportunities that will be abundant in spiritual experiences and will create new pathways for your finances to be abundant too.

856

You are being guided to stop looking ahead and enjoy the scenery of the present moment. Your angels are with you now. Connect with them.

857

You are being guided to remember the power of your mind and emotions. What you focus on and have faith in will be created in your life.

858

You are in a vortex that is rapidly manifesting all that you focus on. Your angels are encouraging you to reconnect with your purpose and their presence in order to manifest positive experiences.

859

You are in a state of extreme spiritual growth at this time. Be aware that your third eye is opening so that you can experience powerful and prophetic visions that will assist you on your journey.

860

Remember that you are sustained by the light and love of God.

861

Your energy and wellness are your greatest assets. Angel wisdom is encouraging you to do all you can to look after your needs at this time.

862

Taking the next steps in relationships is being encouraged at this time. Commitment, vulnerability, and the willingness to be open will all help you to experience the love you deserve.

863

You are attracting opportunities that will light you up and bring you a new sense of love for the world. Take this moment by the hand and move forward.

864

Your angels are encouraging you to tap into the divine guidance that is coming from within. Remember that you are worthy of receiving such information.

865

Angels want you to know that the worst is now behind you with regard to your finances and material stability. Heaven is encouraging you to trust that you are always moving toward abundance and support.

866

Whoah, you are diverting from your intentions and what is of service to you. Angel wisdom is encouraging you to get back on your path and move away from the situations that are causing unnecessary drama in your life.

867

You are experiencing a miraculous moment. Stay connected to love and bring your whole self to everything that you are doing at this time. Your commitment and dedication are being recognized, and heaven is here in support of a positive outcome.

868

All of the bumps on your pathway are being smoothed out. This is a time for plain sailing and a sense of completeness. Your angels are encouraging you to embrace the wholeness of who you have become.

869

Your pathway is leading to a space where you can feel safe enough to reveal the deeper aspects of your soul and psyche. Know that releasing what is within makes space for miracles and healing.

870

God is supporting you as you manifest what you need in order to live a full and joy-filled life.

871

Your angels are encouraging you to turn your attention back to yourself at this time. Stay focused on your growth and you will experience the positivity of your commitment.

872

Your relationships and connections with others are manifesting opportunities for partnership, friendship, and collaboration. Trust that the next phase of your journey involves you sharing space with someone who is as brilliant and talented as you are.

873

Angel wisdom is encouraging you to move away from anything that is distracting you from yourself and the present moment. Step away and reconnect with the magic that is within you.

874

Angels are swirling around you, singing their sweet songs. Know that you are being celebrated and that what you have asked for is being presented to you. Prepare to celebrate in turn.

875

The energy of wonder and celebration is filling your life. You are being encouraged by your angels to look forward with your most positive and loving eyes—you are on the verge of a breakthrough.

876

Angel wisdom is encouraging you to know that the challenges you are facing at this time are opportunities to reclaim your power and wholly accept in your heart that yes, you are ready to be powerful.

877

The angels of blessings are surrounding you now, filling your life with their energy. Open up your heart, mind, and eyes to experience their wonder.

878

Your angels are encouraging you to continually align your thoughts, intentions, and actions with the energy of truth and integrity. Stay focused on your original goal and values and know that they will uncover the answers you need.

879

Your angel guidance is to take some time to retreat back into yourself to restore your mental and emotional wellbeing.

880

God is with and within you. Your path is being cleared and lit up for you.

881

You are being encouraged to take an inventory of how far you have come before you proceed further. Patience is key at this time.

882

The journey you are on wouldn't be what it is if it wasn't for those who lift you up. Angel wisdom is encouraging you to share love and gratitude with those who have supported you this far.

883

Time spent in devotion and prayer will support the expansion of your soul and your experience of feeling supported going forward. Never underestimate your innate connection to God and angels.

884

The angels of freedom are surrounding you, helping you move forward without fears or concerns. You are stepping into a new state of confidence and trust.

885

Your angels are encouraging you to take some time to collect information and study your options before making any changes. Take extra care and assess what is needed before jumping in.

886

Your pathway involves being powerful. Know that your power will always be aligned with the divine plan when you stay focused on offering up truth and doing the right thing for all parties.

887

Angels are now clearing the road ahead and your previous concerns are no longer an issue. Proceed.

888

Your life purpose and your wishes are in alignment. You are doing the right thing and are on the pathway of light.

889

You were born to be a lightworker. Take time to reconnect with the light that you were born to bring to the world.

890

God is supporting you as you uncover your spiritual gifts.

891

You are being encouraged to know that the next step on your journey is about reconnecting with yourself. Take time to come back to yourself.

892

Taking time to care for your needs and being honest about how much you can bring to your relationships are important at this time. Self-care is encouraged.

893

The road ahead is also a reflection of the road within. The more care and energy you put into self-realization, the more light there will be on your journey.

894

Your angels are encouraging you to continually make space in your life to connect with them and open up to their messages. You have a talent for connecting with heaven.

895

Trust that the universe is always delivering what you need in accordance with your intentions and the divine plan. There's nothing you cannot handle.

896

It's important to take some time to review the inspiration and ideas that have been coming to you recently. They are gifts from your soul.

897

You are awakening the Midas touch at this time. All that you touch and all that you focus on will turn to gold.

898

Make sure your hopes, dreams, and wishes are the highest, as your prayers are being answered and your intentions are manifesting now.

899

You are in touch with your Inner Buddha. Connect with that great teacher within and share his messages with the world.

900

God approves of you and your spiritual path.

901

God is grateful that you are finally giving yourself the love and credit you deserve.

902

God is blessing you, your family, and relationships with divine love.

903

Know that God is helping your soul expand so that you can know your angels on a heart level.

904

Angels are in alignment with your soul at this time. Know that the messages you are receiving are coming directly from the heart of God.

905

Embrace the changes that are being presented to you; they are heaven sent.

906

Taking time to move back into a mindset of trust and surrendering all of your concerns to heaven will prepare you to experience the miraculous. Trust in God.

907

The answer you are seeking is already within you. Don't underestimate the wisdom of your soul—listen and you will hear what you need to know.

908

You are being encouraged to realign your pathway with what will light up your soul.

909

Your crown chakra is opening so that you can feel and channel the love of God.

910

You are aligning your energy system with God and the cosmos. Stay light and full of playfulness, as this will keep your vibration high.

911

You are infinitely and cosmically connected to every living thing that is, has been, and ever will be. Connect to the wisdom that you are aligned with at this time.

912

Know that the soul work you are doing is having a positive and healing impact on your life and in particular your relationships and connections with others.

913

You are being encouraged by your angels to trust in the messages and soul-based information coming to you at this time.

914

Make space in your day to dive deep within and invite your angels to come close to you. They are standing by, ready to support you on your journey and in your spiritual development.

915

Your commitment to truth is creating windows of opportunity so that you can feel more in alignment with joy.

916

Your angels are acknowledging your upgraded thinking. You will now reap the benefits of your commitment to a positive and harmonious mind.

917

Your angels are opening the doors to new beginnings and opportunities for you. Embrace change.

918

You are being encouraged to recognize the depth of your spiritual connection and growth. Taking time to see who you have become will prepare you to live a richer and even more magical life.

919

You are experiencing rapid spiritual growth at this time. All darkness is being lifted. Light has come.

920

The angels of romance are entering your life. Prepare to be swept off your feet and enjoy divine connection within relationships and partnerships.

921

The angels of harmony are swirling around you, clearing the energy and restoring serenity in your life.

922

The next phase of your journey will unfold beautifully through your continued self-acceptance. Angel wisdom is encouraging you to give yourself the love you need.

923

You are seeing signs and are in touch with the kingdom of heaven. The key to this connection is the love within you.

924

Angels and archangels are surrounding you and giving you blessings at this time.

925

Angel wisdom is encouraging you to stay focused on the highest and best possible outcome of your current situation. Your prayers and positivity are needed in order for this to happen.

926

Be willing to embrace the changes you are feeling drawn to making. They are not daydreams, but divinely guided inspirations from angels.

927

Know that your prayers have been heard and the answers will come to you according to divine timing.

928

Divine wisdom and guidance are moving through you at this time. What you are hearing is not your imagination but heaven-sent information.

929

You are moving into a peaceful and serene space. Take the opportunity to replenish yourself through mindfulness and self-care.

930

You have God-given healing talents and you are being encouraged to share them with the world in order to experience an increased sense of purpose.

931

Angel wisdom is encouraging you to turn your forgiving heart to yourself. Take time to let go of any grudges or grievances you may be holding on to and experience elevation and connectedness.

932

There is an abundance of love and connection surrounding your relationships at this time.

933

Jesus is here to support your radical ascension. You are going beyond the old stories that once held you back. The chains are now broken and freedom is finally here. Rise up.

934

Your talents, gifts, and light are emerging from within. Angels are encouraging you as you move forward and express who you are.

935

Your angels are encouraging you to celebrate when changes occur around you. Know that everything is unfolding beautifully and as it needs to in order for you to be connected and aligned with your purpose.

936

Continue moving forward, trusting that your angels are with you. Trust will bring the energy of miracles to your pathway and your life.

937

Angel wisdom is encouraging you to connect with the information that is coming to you through your dreams and visions. Powerful messages are being revealed that will support the manifestation of your intentions.

938

Angel wisdom is encouraging you to know that overcoming your current challenges is releasing you from karma and fear connected to past lives. Call on the lords of karma to help you release this for good.

939

You are in touch with the voice and energy of the sacred at this time. Know that you are a vessel for divine love so it is important you care for your body—the vehicle of your soul.

940

God and angels are grateful for the care you are giving yourself at this time.

941

You are being encouraged to know that your angels are always listening to you. You are never alone.

942

You are developing a powerful and profound connection with your guardian angel. Trust what you are hearing and experiencing.

943

You are surrounded and supported by your guides.

944

Angels are helping you uncover and recover gifts that have been lost or forgotten. Psychic insights and visions are highly likely at this time.

945

Archangels are protecting you as you unlock the deeper aspects of your soul and your soul's work.

946

The angels of balance are encouraging you to make sure your life has consistency and connection. Step away from draining situations and focus on what gives you life.

947

The energy of intention is important at this time. Your intentions are creating your experiences, so your angels are encouraging you to be clear about what you want and how you want to live going forward.

948

Know that you are experiencing powerful insights and downloads with regard to your life path. The truths you need are now being revealed to you.

949

The Holy Spirit is filling up the cup of your heart until it is overflowing. Know that you are deserving of miracles.

950

The changes that have been occurring have been created and curated by God. Have faith in the bigger picture.

951

You are being guided to be the master of your own mind. Focus on what you desire and set your sights high.

952

You are being guided to face anything that is standing in your way, because once you have done so, the magic you have been dreaming of will be revealed. Stay focused.

953

Expanding your soul requires you to do some diving within and facing fear. But know that you are on the verge of major spiritual changes. Soon you will be flying high.

954

Your angels are encouraging you to care for yourself as you move through changes. Be compassionate to yourself and give yourself credit when required.

955

You are unlocking a profound truth and this is creating powerful changes that will unleash your spiritual self. Reveal your gifts to experience abundance.

956

The hard work that you have put in is now paying off and a sense of balance is being restored. What you give—and have given—you will get.

957

Stay devoted to your dreams, visions, and intentions—you are closer than you have ever been to seeing them manifest. Know that your commitment will pay off.

958

You are surrounded by supreme protection and are being encouraged to know that you are safe even if things get bumpy. There may be some turbulence at this time, but soon everything will be smooth once more.

959

You are being called to action. Heaven is guiding you to take your purpose and share it with the world. You have an opportunity to lead by example. Take it.

960

God is encouraging you to know that the inner work you have been doing has cleared old blockages in your energy and your family lineage. Old wounds have been healed.

961

Your light is being activated. Shine with all of your might and know that you are aligned with the highest.

962

Take time to consider all those you love and are connected with before setting any intentions for your future. You are being guided to become more aware of who and what is important.

963

Emerge from the cave. You have something important to share. Follow your inner call. Let the teacher out.

964

You are making powerful psychic connections at this time. Your angels are speaking through your intuition and it's important to trust what you are hearing.

965

You are being guided to stop being so attached to the material at this time, as you are blocking the energy of abundance that is trying to bless your life. Surrender and let the magic in.

966

In order to increase your awareness, be radically honest with yourself.

967

Your truth is your teacher. Know that when you stand up for what you believe in, you will manifest experiences that will allow you to be more supported by God and angels.

968

Your angels are encouraging you to reveal your sensitive side. You are in a space of radical self-acceptance now. Let what's good about you be seen and accepted by others too.

969

Your soul is curating opportunities for you to experience powerful shifts at this time, as your energy is golden and aligned with the energies of divine alchemy and magic.

970

God is encouraging you to know that the next phase of your journey requires deep self-love and acceptance.

971

Divine guidance is encouraging you to choose loving thoughts. Recognize your own divine worth. Love is yours to have, share, and experience.

972

Taking time to recharge is important for you now. You are being guided to honor your sensitivity, too, as being able to manage your vulnerable side will help you support others.

973

Angels and ascended masters are placing a golden light of wisdom around you. You are being guided to realize that the answer you are seeking is actually within you.

974

Your angels are encouraging you to know that you are at the end of one phase or cycle and are asking you to trust them as they guide you to the next. Old illusions are being revealed and released now.

975

Trust in the power of heaven. Your angels are close to you.

976

You are being encouraged to remember the universe is with and within you. When you remember how connected you are, a cloak of spiritual protection will hold you in a space of love.

977

The power and energy of life and magic are moving through your life now. Call for the miracles you need and prepare to receive them immediately.

978

Your *dharma*, your path of righteousness, is unfolding excellently. Take one step at a time. Happiness awaits.

979

You are releasing ties, bonds, chains, and karmic attachments that have held you back from stepping into a place of power and light.

980

God is directing you on your journey. Know that your path is in alignment with divine love.

981

You are rediscovering your own power and light. Welcome home to the real you.

982

You are experiencing relationship harmony and peace at this time. All your previous concerns and challenges are being washed away and replaced with love and acceptance.

983

Reconnect with Earth energy. The next phase of your journey requires you to be grounded.

984

Your angel team is encouraging you to speak up and to make sure that your heartfelt truth is heard. Be radically honest—this is required if you are to be respected.

985

Justice and divine order are being brought to your current situation. Angel guidance is encouraging you to do the right thing for everyone involved.

986

You are in a powerful space for higher learning to unfold. Know that your current experience is a powerful teaching moment.

987

Angel guidance is encouraging you to stay calm and trust that everything is unfolding as it needs to in order for you to experience abundance and magic.

988

Your angels never want you to underestimate the significance and power of your life. You have something special to share.

989

You are in touch with something important. Obstacles are being cleared and challenges released, and you are moving into a space of personal transcendence.

990

You are on the path of light and love. God is encouraging you to remember you are never condemned and always loved, forgiven, and encouraged.

991

Reconnect with heaven. Take time for prayer and contemplation. Ask and you shall receive.

992

Know that heaven is also within your relationships and any previous challenges are now being cleared so that you can love fearlessly.

993

Divine intervention is occurring. Know that you are being guided toward happiness and purpose.

994

Angels are supporting you as you unlock and connect with divine vision. Be willing to see the world through the eyes of love and forgiveness.

995

The universe knows exactly what you need in order to rise up. Your process of ascension is moving forward at this time and you are rising above darkness.

996

Waves of inspiration and love are moving through you and emerging from you now. Share your gifts with the world in order to experience grace.

997

Your life is aligned with your purpose and with higher purpose. Nothing you have done up to this point has been by accident. Now experience the magic of who you are.

998

Your intentions to grow and heal have been manifested. Rejoice in who you have become.

999

The Divine Mother Mary is supporting you as you move back to a sense of wholeness. Welcome home to your heart.

Afterword

Remember, there are many angels surrounding the Earth. You have one or more guardian angels with you at all times. You are their purpose. They want nothing more than for you to feel safe, guided, and guarded. They take every opportunity to remind you that they are close by and can support you with their miracles. The reason that they are with you is because you are love and you deserve to experience love.

Whatever number messages you are receiving, trust that your angels are on standby, waiting to help you, and lead you to freedom and love. They are only a prayer away. And no prayer remains unanswered.

May your angels keep you safe and protect you on your journey.

ABOUT THE AUTHOR

Bob Rafferty

Kyle Gray has had spiritual encounters from an early age. When he was just four years old, his grandmother's soul visited him from beyond the grave.

Growing up, Kyle always had an ability to hear, feel and see what goes beyond the natural senses which, in his teens, led him to discovering the power and love of angels.

Now Kyle is one of the most hip and sought-after experts in his field. With his unique ability to stay grounded and keep it real, he reintroduces the angels and spirituality in an accessible way to a modern audience and makes ancient spiritual knowledge relevant to today's reader.

Kyle has appeared on *Loose Women* and *This Morning*, and featured on BBC Radio. He speaks all over the world, and his talks in the UK and Europe have been known to sell out. Kyle is based in Glasgow, Scotland, and is the author of six books and three oracle card decks.

kylegrayuk

@kylegrayuk

@kylegrayuk

www.kylegray.co.uk

'The gateways to wisdom and knowledge are always open.'

Louise Hay

Praise for Kyle Gray

"Kyle Gray is an incredibly talented medium and guide for a new generation of spiritual seekers and the already converted."

Gabrielle Bernstein, *New York Times* bestselling author of *The Universe Has Your Back* and *Miracles Now*

"Each week in Woman's World *magazine, Kyle Gray helps readers interpret the divine messages they receive from the angels. Here, in the same simple, clear language, he decodes the messages angels send hidden in number sequences that repeatedly pop up in our daily lives. An eye-opening, inspirational, potentially life-changing read!"*

Woman's World magazine

"Kyle Gray is one of the world's most incredibly gifted angel communicators. I have seen him work and he is authentic, intelligent, and deeply compassionate. I highly recommend him and all his creations!"

Colette Baron-Reid, international bestselling oracle expert

"I had full-bodied chills. Kyle Gray is the hottest, hippest medium who translates the wisdom of the angels in the most loving and relatable way possible. I couldn't recommend his brilliant spiritual gifts more."

Meggan Watterson, author of *Mary Magdalene Revealed*

"I adore Kyle Gray. He helps you to reconnect with all that is wanting to rise up within you, be available to the benevolent support that already surrounds you and release what is wanting to fall away with grace."

REBECCA CAMPBELL, AUTHOR OF *LIGHT IS THE NEW BLACK* AND *RISE SISTER RISE*

"Kyle Gray changes lives."

THE SUN

"Kyle Gray is now one of the most successful 'angel readers' in the UK."

PSYCHOLOGIES MAGAZINE

"Kyle Gray is a natural down-to-earth psychic; I found him to be startlingly accurate. He has a remarkable spiritual connection."

DR DAVID R. HAMILTON PHD, BESTSELLING AUTHOR OF *HOW YOUR MIND CAN HEAL YOUR BODY*

"Kyle's an expert in his field."

SPIRIT & DESTINY MAGAZINE

"You will feel fully supported with Kyle and your angels by your side, celebrating your every breakthrough."

SANDY C. NEWBIGGING, BESTSELLING AUTHOR OF *MIND CALM*

"The hottest name in spirituality!"

SOUL & SPIRIT MAGAZINE